IMAGES
of America

LEGENDS OF
WESTWOOD VILLAGE
CEMETERY

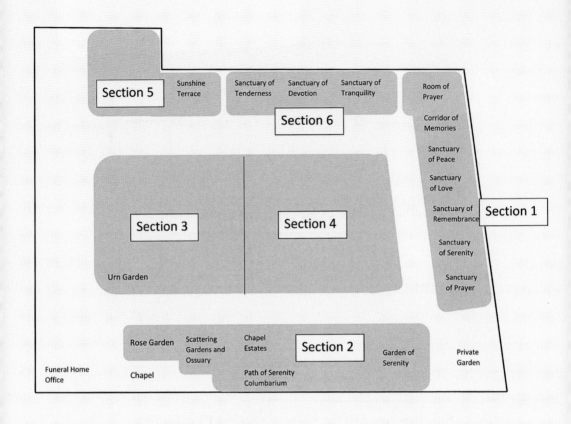

		Sunshine Terrace	Sanctuary of Tenderness	Sanctuary of Devotion	Sanctuary of Tranquility	Room of Prayer

Section 5

Section 6

Corridor of Memories

Sanctuary of Peace

Sanctuary of Love

Sanctuary of Remembrance | **Section 1**

Section 3

Section 4

Sanctuary of Serenity

Urn Garden

Sanctuary of Prayer

Rose Garden | Scattering Gardens and Ossuary | Chapel Estates

Section 2

Garden of Serenity

Private Garden

Funeral Home Office

Chapel

Path of Serenity Columbarium

MAP OF WESTWOOD VILLAGE CEMETERY. This map, created by coauthor Phil Lantis, shows the cemetery divided into six sections to make the graves written about in this book easier to find. Our trip around Westwood Cemetery begins in Section 1 at the crypt of Marilyn Monroe, at the northeast corner of the cemetery, and continues to the other sections in a clockwise direction.

ON THE COVER: Members of the paparazzi stand shoulder to shoulder, overlooking the funeral of Hollywood superstar Marilyn Monroe at Westwood Village Cemetery in Los Angeles on August 8, 1962. (Courtesy of Marc Wanamaker, Bison Archives)

IMAGES
of America

LEGENDS OF
WESTWOOD VILLAGE
CEMETERY

E.J. Stephens, Kim Stephens, and Phil Lantis

ARCADIA
PUBLISHING

Published by Arcadia Publishing
Charleston, South Carolina

Printed in the United States of America

Library of Congress Control Number: 2023947667

For all general information, please contact Arcadia Publishing:
Telephone 843-853-2070
Fax 843-853-0044
E-mail sales@arcadiapublishing.com

Visit us on the Internet at www.arcadiapublishing.com

Dedicated to the many thousands of lives who are memorialized at Westwood Village Cemetery. We wish we had room within these pages to celebrate them all.

CONTENTS

ACKNOWLEDGMENTS

Kimi and E.J. would like to again thank Marc Wanamaker for all his support on this book (and several others). It would not have been possible without images from his amazing Bison Archives. We would also like to thank our friends and family members, especially Mariah and Dylan, who made this journey so enjoyable. And thanks to our buddy Phil for all the great work on this book and on all of our other fun pursuits. (You can learn about one of these projects at www.newhallywoodfilmfest.org.)

Phil would like to thank his wife, Nancy, and children, George and Sally, for putting up with his mood swings while finishing this book.

All pictures are courtesy of Bison Archives unless specified otherwise.

INTRODUCTION

When the legendary Hollywood actress and sex symbol Marilyn Monroe died in August 1962, one of the reasons her ex-husband Joe DiMaggio chose to inter her remains at Pierce Brothers Westwood Village Memorial Park and Mortuary was because it was not known as a celebrity cemetery. Much has changed in the intervening six decades. Thanks to Marilyn, Westwood has gone from being simply a serene urban burial ground tucked behind tall buildings to becoming *the* celebrity cemetery of choice.

Many people chose Westwood as their place of eternal rest to be near Marilyn, whose grave is a major tourist attraction in Los Angeles. Of the 344 "famous" people that Westwood has listed in findagrave.com, virtually every one of them died after the blonde superstar. The trend started with Darbi Winters, whose crypt is one space up and to the right of Marilyn's. Winters was a 16-year-old aspiring actress who worshipped the blonde bombshell and wished to be buried near her after she died. Tragically, she waited less than three months after Marilyn's death to have her wish fulfilled after being murdered by her stepfather. It was the start of a trend. In 2017, the body of Hugh Hefner, the man who used a nude photo of Marilyn to launch *Playboy* magazine in 1953, reportedly paid a hefty fee to be placed in the crypt to her left. It gets weirder. When Los Angeles businessman Richard Poncher died in 1986, his final wish was to be placed in the crypt immediately above and have his body turned over so he could face Marilyn for eternity.

While other graveyards in the Los Angeles area like Forest Lawn and Hollywood Forever may have a higher number of famous internments, both are many times larger than Westwood's two picturesque acres. Within Westwood's walls, the graves of many of the most famous people who ever lived can be found. It's safe to say that for its size, there is nowhere on Earth with more notable "permanent residents" than Westwood Cemetery.

Since Westwood is nestled between Beverly Hills, Bel Air, and Santa Monica in the heart of Los Angeles's trendy west side, it's not surprising that most residents here achieved fame in the entertainment industry. In addition to the aforementioned Monroe, the cemetery houses the remains of an embarrassment of riches of household names. Just some include Patty Andrews, Eve Arden, Lew Ayres, Jim Backus, Richard Basehart, Peter Bogdanovich, Ray Bradbury, Fanny Brice, Les Brown, Sebastian Cabot, Truman Capote, Harry Carey Jr., John Cassavetes, James Coburn, Jackie Collins, Richard Conte, Tim Conway, Bob Crane, Rodney Dangerfield, Richard Dawson, Don DeFore, Kirk Douglas, Dominique Dunne, Will and Ariel Durant, Peter Falk, Farrah Fawcett, Marion Jones Farquhar, June Foray, Eva Gabor, Christopher George, Merv Griffin, Jonathan Harris, Heyedeh, Hugh Hefner, Florence Henderson, James Wong Howe, Jim Hutton, Nunnally Johnson, Louis Jourdan, Brian Keith, Stan Kenton, Jack Klugman, Don Knotts, Burt Lancaster, Peggy Lee, Janet Leigh, Jack Lemmon, Oscar Levant, Robert Loggia, Karl Malden, Dean Martin, Walter Matthau, Rod McKuen, Lewis Milestone, David Nelson, Lloyd Nolan, Robert Newton, Carroll O'Connor, Heather O'Rourke, Bettie Page, Wolfgang Petersen, Gregor Piatigorsky, Donna Reed, Buddy Rich, Minnie Riperton, Doris Roberts, Wayne Rogers, George C. Scott, Sidney Sheldon,

Robert Stack, Dorothy Stratten, Alvin Toffler, Mel Tormé, Josef Von Sternberg, Harry Warren, Joe Weider, Cornel Wilde, Billy Wilder, Carl Wilson, Natalie Wood, Darryl F. Zanuck, Frank Zappa, and incredibly, hundreds more.

Most of these names are familiar to anyone who has spent time in front of a radio, television set, or movie screen. But Westwood is also the final resting place for dozens of character actors of the past whose faces, rather than names, were more familiar to audiences. A few examples are Connie Hines, who played the role of Carol Post on *Mr. Ed*, and Lloyd Bochner, who learned too late the true purpose of the "To Serve Man" book on *The Twilight Zone*. Allan Melvin, who played Sam the Butcher on *The Brady Bunch* and provided the voice for Magilla Gorilla, is here. So is Jonathan Harris, better known as Dr. Zachary Smith from *Lost In Space*, along with Ed Lauter, Burt Reynolds's nemesis in *The Longest Yard* (1974). Ruth McDevitt, famous for dozens of "little old lady" roles, is here, as is Doris Moran, wife of producer Benedict Bogeus, who appeared in a few films in the 1940s and was a pin-up girl during World War II. Jim Hutton, the father of actor Timothy Hutton, who played Ellery Queen on television, is here, as is Jeff Morris, the owner of Bob's Country Bunker in 1980's *The Blues Brothers*. Paul Gleason, better known as Principal Vernon from 1985's iconic *The Breakfast Club* is here, as is Richard Anderson, who played Oscar Goldman on both *The Six Million Dollar Man* and *The Bionic Woman*.

The roster of noted film directors in Westwood is truly astonishing, with many among the most revered in film history. This list includes Ken Annakin, Jack Arnold, Hy Averback, Peter Bogdanovich, John Cassavetes, Phil Karlson, Louis King, Alexander Mackendrick, Lewis Milestone, Wolfgang Petersen, Ben Roberts, Herbert Ross, Franklin Schaffner, Ernest B. Schoedsack, Frank Tuttle, Josef von Sternberg, Billy Wilder, and Edward Yang, among others.

Many of the actors, writers, and crew members now interred in Westwood were employed at one time or another by the dozens of producers that are here, like James Aubrey, William J. Bell, Benedict Bogeaus, John J. Carsey, Chuck Fries, Harold Hecht, Ross Hunter, Alan W. Livingston, Samuel Marx, Richard Charles King, G. David Schine, Ray Stark, William C. Thomas, Darryl F. Zanuck, and many, many others.

Several music catalogs could be filled by the composers of Westwood Cemetery. You may not be familiar with the name Milton Ager, but you certainly know his songs "Ain't She Sweet?" and "Happy Days Are Here Again." Italian composer Mario Castelnuovo-Tedesco is here. So is Sammy Cahn. His songs were nominated for Oscars over 30 times, and he took home the award for four of them, including "High Hopes" and "My Kind of Town." Songwriting partners Ray Evans and Jay Livingston are both here. They wrote 26 songs that sold over a million copies, including the Christmastime staple, "Silver Bells." Sandy Courage is also buried here. His name may not ring a bell, but the theme he composed for *Star Trek* is familiar to science-fiction fans across the galaxy. Legendary Harry Warren is interred at Westwood. He wrote dozens of eminently hummable tunes nearly a century ago, like "I Only Have Eyes for You," "42nd Street," "Jeepers Creepers," "Lullaby of Broadway," and "On the Atchison, Topeka, and the Santa Fe." His crypt, in the Sanctuary of Tenderness, is inscribed with the first few notes of "You'll Never Know," another of his many classics.

Westwood is filled with famous musicians, singers, and bandleaders from the past, like Patti Andrews, one-third of the Andrews Sisters, who sold over 75 million records. Others include Les Brown, drummer Stan Kenton, Peggy Lee, Oscar Levant, Patti Page, Buddy Rich, and Mel "The Velvet Fog" Tormé. Eileen Barton is here. She scored a million-selling single in 1950 with "If I Knew You Were Coming, I'd've Baked a Cake." Minnie Riperton, the mother of comedienne Maya Rudolph, is also here. She demonstrated her five-octave vocal range beautifully on the 1975 hit "Lovin' You." Cellist Gregor Piatigorsky is buried in Westwood. So are the Iranian sisters Heyedeh and Mahasti Dadebala, and opera stars Helen Traubel, Miliza Korjus, and Gitta Alper (whose crypt is only inches away from Marilyn's).

Rock 'n' roll is well represented at Westwood. Beach Boy Carl Wilson is here as is punk singer Bobbi Brat. Danny Sugerman, who managed the legendary rock group The Doors is here, and so is Felix Venable, a filmmaker who was a friend of Jim Morrison. Geoff Emerick, who was an English sound engineer is in Section 4. As a teenager, he worked on the albums *Revolver*, *Sgt. Pepper's Lonely*

Hearts Club Band, and *Abbey Road* for a little British band called The Beatles. The graves of rock legends Roy Orbison and Frank Zappa, whose burial sites deserve statues, are located near each other in unmarked graves.

Westwood Cemetery is also home to dozens of legends of the written word. The crypt of Truman Capote, who wrote *In Cold Blood*, is steps away from Jackie Collins, the author of 500 million novels in print. Robert Bloch, the author of *Psycho*, is here, as is Alvin Toffler, author of *Future Shock*. Will and Ariel Durant, who created the 11-volume series *The Story of Civilization*, are next to one another under a shady tree. Ray Bradbury, the author of *The Martian Chronicles*, *Fahrenheit 451*, and dozens of other science-fiction and fantasy classics, can be found near the fountains. This is in addition to the dozens of award-winning screenwriters interred here, like Richard Baer, Harry Essex, Nunnally Johnson, Ernest Lehman, Richard Levinson, Frank Pierson, Ben Roberts, Ruth Rose, and Sidney Sheldon.

The passing of some of Westwood's residents silenced the voices of several beloved cartoon characters like Mr. Magoo, Wilma Flintstone, Mr. Limpet, Manny, Snooty Iris, Clark Kent, Duchess, Bagheera, Percival C. McLeash, Magilla Gorilla, Henry J. Waternoose, Big Bad Wolf, Barnacle Boy, and Mikey Blumberg. The talented actors who voiced these characters, Jim Backus, June Foray, Don Knotts, Jonathan Harris, Queenie Leonard, Danny Dark, Eva Gabor, Sebastian Cabot, George C. Scott, Allan Melvin, James Coburn, Billy Bletcher, Tim Conway, and Jason Phillip Davis, are all buried at Westwood.

Because Hollywood is a company town, it is not surprising that many of the inhabitants of Westwood have interesting connections. Jack Lemmon and Walter Matthau are near one another, which is appropriate, as they were often paired on screen. Lemmon is also near Billy Wilder, who directed him (and Marilyn) in *Some Like It Hot* (1959). Lewis Milestone, who won an Oscar for directing the Best Picture–winning 1930 film *All Quiet on the Western Front*, is buried near actor Lew Ayres, who starred in the film. Eva Gabor and Eddie Albert, the stars of *Green Acres*, are both here. As are Bob Crane, Richard Dawson, and Sigrid Valdis from *Hogan's Heroes*. Richard Basehart, who played Admiral Nelson in TV's *Voyage to the Bottom of the Sea*, is here. He starred in a film called *Time Limit* in 1957, which happens to be the only movie that Westwood neighbor Karl Malden ever directed. Don Knotts and Tim Conway, the stars of *The Apple Dumpling Gang* movies of the 1970s, are both in Westwood at opposite ends of the cemetery. The same is true for George C. Scott, who famously won, and then turned down, the Best Actor Oscar in 1970 for *Patton*, and Franklin Schaffner, who won (and kept) the Oscar for directing the same film. Karl Malden, who also appeared in *Patton*, is buried next to Scott. *Family Affair* stars Brian Keith and Sebastian Cabot are interred only steps from each other. And while it's uncertain if actors Janet Leigh and Jack Klugman were ever closely linked in life, they certainly are in the afterlife, because today their graves are next to each other.

Certain films are the source of numerous connections at Westwood. *Sweet Smell of Success* (1957) was directed by Alexander Mackendrick, produced by Harold Hecht, starred Burt Lancaster, was written by Ernest Lehman, and featured James Wong Howe as the cinematographer. Today, these five men are all buried at Westwood. Another interesting connection comes from the 1933 film *King Kong*. Fay Wray is buried at Hollywood Forever Cemetery*, but Robert Armstrong, her costar in the film, is at Westwood, as are codirector Ernest Schoedsack and his wife, Ruth Rose Schoedsack, who wrote the screenplay. Actress Helen Mack is also interred here. She appeared in the film's sequel, *Son of Kong*, also released in 1933.

And while Westwood is heavily populated with award-winning actors and directors, it is also the final home of filmmakers who are better known to *Mystery Science Theater 3000* fans than to TCM aficionados. Near Don Knotts is the grave of Loretta Funk Hadler, who appeared in Ed Wood's *Bride of the Monster*, and Joanna Lee, who starred in Wood's schlocky magnum opus, *Plan Nine from Outer Space*. Coleman Francis, who directed the deliciously bad *Beast of Yucca Flats*, is here as well. And Edith Massey, John Waters's "egg lady," had her ashes scattered in the Rose Garden.

The business world is also well represented in Westwood. Former Los Angeles Rams owner Georgia Frontiere is here near hotelier Arnold Kirkeby and billionaire oilmen Marvin Davis and

Waite Phillips. As previously noted, talk show host Merv Griffin, another billionaire, is here. So is Armand Hammer, who is interred in an above-ground mausoleum just a few hundred yards from an art museum that bears his name.

Although this is Hollywood, not all the lives featured within these pages concluded with happy Hollywood endings. Many succumbed to accidents, diseases, suicides, drug overdoses, and murders. This is true of Marilyn Monroe, Natalie Wood, Bob Crane, Dorothy Stratten, Hugh O'Connor, Dominique Dunne, Coleman Francis, Heather O'Rourke, and Brian Keith and his daughter Daisy. Some lesser-known lives here ended tragically as well, like Ronald Hughes, who was rumored to be murdered by the Manson Family. The body of Robert Gottschalk, the founder of Panavision, rests in a tomb in the Sanctuary of Tenderness. He was stabbed to death in 1983. The graves of *The French Connection* (1971) producer G. David Schine, his wife (and former Miss Universe) Hillevi, and their son Berndt are here in Section 4 under a single headstone inscribed with the date June 19, 1996, the day of their fatal plane crash.

A few other lives in Westwood are also linked by tragedy. The cemetery houses the graves of Dominique Dunne, who was murdered by her boyfriend at age 22, and Heather O'Rourke, who died at age 12. Both costarred in the *Poltergeist* movies of the 1980s. Stranger still, the ashes of character actors Victor Killian and Charles Wagenheim were scattered here in 1979 after both were murdered at nearly the same time in the same manner. Ironically, both appeared together in an episode of *All in the Family* (with fellow Westwood resident Carroll O'Connor), which was broadcast just days after their deaths.

But not all is grim at Westwood. Many of the world's greatest comics are also interred here. Rodney Dangerfield's grave is in a prime spot near the chapel. A comedian to the end, his epitaph reads, "There Goes the Neighborhood." Billy Wilder's epitaph evokes the final line of his film *Some Like It Hot*. It reads, "I'm a Writer, but then Nobody's Perfect." Nearby, television host Merv Griffin's tombstone reads, "I Will Not Be Right Back After This Message." Stand-up comedian Kip Addotta is buried nearby, as is funnyman Tim Conway of *The Carol Burnett Show* fame. So is Don Knotts, who, as Deputy Barney Fife on *The Andy Griffith Show*, was one of television's all-time funniest and best-loved characters.

Some of the most humorous epitaphs come from non-famous residents. A woman named Maggie is described on her tomb as a "Chicago Lass with Irish Sass." Another one nearby reads, "Don't Forget to Feed the Cats." Perhaps the most memorable epitaph comes from the crypt of a man named Steviedon Cochran, who is entombed in the next section over from Marilyn. His helpful epitaph, which has undoubtedly aided dozens of lost fans, reads, "Marilyn is around the corner."

Westwood Cemetery is not just a place for the dead, but a serene, welcoming, contemplative spot for the living, with landscaped graves and outdoor crypts that are easily accessible to visitors. We hope you find the stories in the following pages to be interesting and respectful accounts of the lives of some of the extraordinary people housed within.

E.J. and Kim Stephens and Phil Lantis
Santa Clarita, California, December 2023

*Readers can learn more about Hollywood Forever Cemetery in Arcadia Publishing's Images of America book *Legends of Hollywood Forever Cemetery*, written by coauthors E.J. and Kim Stephens.

One

SECTION 1

Westwood Cemetery is small in size with several areas, each with a different name. This breakdown can prove difficult for the casual visitor. To help eliminate confusion, the authors have divided the property into six sections. Since Westwood's history of celebrity burials began with Marilyn Monroe in 1962, it is only fitting that the tour begins on the cemetery's northeast side at her lipstick-covered crypt, which is in a section of outdoor tombs officially named the Corridor of Memories. This is the start of Section 1. It continues on around to the Private Garden far to the right.

The walls surrounding Monroe hold the crypts of such notables as Hugh Hefner, Darbi Winters, Jay C. Flippen, Ross Hunter, Gitta Alper, and Steve Ihnat.

Moving clockwise from Marilyn's crypt is the private Room of Prayer, which houses the cremated remains of actors Robert Stack and Charles Aidman, writer Robert Bloch, and burlesque queen Dixie Evans. Poet Rod McKuen's crypt is in a wall outside and to the right of the Room of Prayer. Further down, inside the Sanctuary of Love, are the crypts of crooner Dean Martin, composer Oscar Levant, and tennis great Marion Jones Farquhar.

Continuing on is the private crypt of Waite Phillips, the founder of Phillips Petroleum. Next door, in the Sanctuary of Remembrance, are the crypts of composers Roger Edens and Leonard Gershe, opera singer Helen Traubel, Hollywood super-agent Sam Jaffe, director Sidney Lanfield and his wife, silent star Shirley Mason, filmmaker Felix Venable, director Coleman Frances, actress Winifred Westover, character actors Rennie Riano, Cecil Kellaway, and Percy Helton, film editor George Boemler, and the site of director Josef von Sternberg's first Westwood burial.

Actor John Boles, who played Victor Moritz in 1931's horror classic *Frankenstein*, is in a wall crypt around the corner in the Sanctuary of Serenity. On the opposite wall are the crypts of actor Wayne Rogers of M*A*S*H fame, and those of actors Les Tremayne and Robert Loggia. Circling on around past private mausoleums marked Mancuso and Goldberg (which houses producer Leonard Goldberg) in the Sanctuary of Prayer are the outdoor crypts of voice actor Jason Phillip Davis, comedian Tim Conway, businesswoman Georgia Frontiere, and director Josef von Sternberg's second and final Westwood resting place (at least, for now). Bodybuilding promoter Joe Weider is here in an unmarked crypt, and Alan Livingston is interred in a private underground mausoleum located beneath this section.

ROBERT BLOCH (1917–1994), ROOM OF PRAYER. If there had not been a Robert Bloch, there would never have been a Norman Bates. Bloch's best-known work was the novel *Psycho*, which Alfred Hitchcock turned into the horror classic of the same name in 1960, starring Anthony Perkins as the psychopathic killer Norman Bates and Westwood neighbor Janet Leigh as one of his victims. Bloch was a prolific writer of science-fiction, horror, crime, and fantasy novels. Horror-fantasy writer H.P. Lovecraft, with whom Bloch corresponded as a teenager, was one of his main influences.

JOHN BOLES (1895–1969), SANCTUARY OF SERENITY. Actor-singer John Boles achieved his greatest success playing the role of Victor Moritz in the Universal horror classic *Frankenstein* (1931). Boles, who was born in Texas, began acting during the silent era. His melodic voice carried his career into talkies where he sang in some of the earliest musicals of Warner Bros. and RKO. During his long career, he starred opposite some of Hollywood's top leading ladies, like Gloria Swanson, Bebe Daniels, Barbara Stanwyck, and Shirley Temple. Above is a still from *The Love of Sanya* (1927), with John Boles and Gloria Swanson.

TIM CONWAY (1933–2019), SANCTUARY OF PRAYER. Thomas Daniel "Tim" Conway hilariously lit up movie and television screens in over 100 roles during a long career. Conway created numerous hilarious characters, like the gullible Ensign Parker on *McHale's Navy*, the bumbling criminal-wannabe in the *Apple Dumpling Gang* films (which paired him with Westwood neighbor Don Knotts), and as "Dorf" on several direct-to-video sports comedies. But to most fans, he will be best remembered for his hilarious creations on the sketch comedy series *The Carol Burnett Show*, which not only cracked up viewers at home, but also his costars on stage (most often Harvey Korman). Conway won six Emmys during his career, four for his work with Carol Burnett. Born in Ohio, Conway began his career as a popular disc jockey and television comedian in Cleveland. Rose Marie of *The Dick Van Dyke Show* discovered him on a visit to Cleveland and helped Conway land a role on *The Steve Allen Show*. This led to an acting gig on *McHale's Navy*, followed by his time with Carol Burnett. Conway was also a successful voice actor, most notably as "Barnacle Boy" on *SpongeBob SquarePants*. He died in 2019 at the age of 85.

ROGER EDENS (1905–1970) AND LEONARD GERSHE (1922–2002), SANCTUARY OF REMEMBRANCE. Texas-born Roger Edens first came to Hollywood to compose music for Ethel Merman films. At MGM, he became an integral part of Arthur Freed's production team. This group was responsible for several musical hits in the 1940s and 1950s, like *Meet Me in St. Louis* (1944), *Easter Parade* (1948), *On the Town* (1949), *Show Boat* (1951), *Singin' in the Rain* (1952), and *The Band Wagon* (1953). Edens was in a long-term relationship with lyricist Leonard Gershe, and they are entombed together in the Sanctuary of Remembrance.

MARION JONES FARQUHAR (1879–1965), SANCTUARY OF LOVE. Near Dean Martin is the crypt of International Tennis Hall of Fame member Marion Jones Farquhar. Farquhar won the singles titles in 1899 and 1902 at the US Championships. In 1900, she became the first American woman to win an Olympic medal. She was also the first non-British woman to play at Wimbledon. Farquhar was the daughter of a Nevada senator who founded the city of Santa Monica, California. A woman of many talents, she lived for years in New York City, where she was a violinist and voice coach. (Photograph by E.J. Stephens.)

COLEMAN FRANCIS (1919–1973), SANCTUARY OF REMEMBRANCE. In the Sanctuary of Remembrance is the small memorial to the man who may be the most maligned movie director of all time, not named Ed Wood. Coleman Francis was one of the thousands of Okies who resettled in Southern California during the Dust Bowl. He played several minor roles in forgettable films before partnering with welder Tony Cardoza to create *The Beast of Yucca Flats* (1961), *The Skydivers* (1963), and *Red Zone Cuba* (1966), arguably three of the worst movies ever made. Bad reviews and poor health took their toll on Francis. He died mysteriously in 1973 due to either homicide or, more likely, suicide. He was only 53 at the time of his death.

GEORGIA FRONTIERE (1927–2008), SANCTUARY OF PRAYER. For many years, Georgia Frontiere was the only female owner of an NFL team, the Los Angeles/St. Louis Rams. Originally from St. Louis, Frontiere moved to Miami in the late 1950s where she hosted her own television interview show and performed as a nightclub singer. When husband number four (of six) died in 1979, she inherited the Rams. Her three-decade tenure as an NFL owner was fairly successful, as the Rams made the playoffs during fourteen seasons, reached the Super Bowl three times, and won the big game in 1999, four years after her controversial decision to move the team from Los Angeles to St. Louis.

HUGH HEFNER (1926–2017), CORRIDOR OF MEMORIES. Hugh Hefner was never far from controversy from age 26, when he founded *Playboy* magazine, until his death 65 years later. To some, "Hef" was a champion of First Amendment rights and stood at the vanguard of the sexual revolution. To others, he was an exploiter of women who helped perpetuate sexist stereotypes. *Playboy*, a magazine that promoted a jet-set lifestyle that was known partly for its cutting-edge journalism but mostly for its pictures of beautiful nude women, began in December 1953 with $8,000 Hef scrounged up from friends and relatives.

HUGH HEFNER (1926–2017), CORRIDOR OF MEMORIES. The first issue of *Playboy* featured a nude centerfold of Westwood's Marilyn Monroe. Hefner reportedly paid $600 for the rights. That issue sold 50,000 copies and launched the *Playboy* empire, which included the magazine—selling seven million copies a month at its peak—Playboy Clubs, and a cable television channel. Hef lived and worked in the Playboy Mansion in Holmby Hills, California, where dozens of "Playmates" partied continuously with the glitterati of Hollywood. Hefner was married several times and had numerous relationships with his Playmates. When he died, his body was placed inside the crypt immediately to Marilyn's left, thereby bringing him full circle to be next to the woman who helped create his empire.

17

Ross Hunter (1920–1996), Corridor of Memories. Martin Fuss from Cleveland became Ross Hunter when he began a career in B-musicals in the 1940s. After a short acting career, he switched his focus to producing. His breakthrough hit came in 1954 with *Magnificent Obsession*, starring Rock Hudson. Several rom-coms followed, including *Pillow Talk* (1959), again with Rock Hudson. By 1965, 32 of his films made over the previous 11 years grossed a combined $150 million. In 1970, Hunter produced *Airport*, with Westwood neighbors Burt Lancaster and Dean Martin, which earned a Best Picture nomination. Moving to television, Hunter's last project was a 1979 movie starring Westwooder Donna Reed.

Sidney Lanfield (1898–1972) and Shirley Mason (1901–1979), Sanctuary of Remembrance. Silent film actress Shirley Mason, along with sisters Edna Flugrath and Viola Dana, were the daughters of a stage mother who forced them into acting. Each of the girls made it big in Hollywood during the 1920s. Mason appeared in over 100 films between 1910 and 1929. She was married for decades to director Sidney Lanfield, who gained fame by directing Bob Hope in several popular comedies. He also directed *Hound of the Baskervilles* (1939), the first in a series of renowned Sherlock Holmes films, starring Basil Rathbone and Nigel Bruce. This is a photograph of Shirley Mason and her stage mother.

OSCAR LEVANT (1906–1972), SANCTUARY OF LOVE. Musician, composer, and actor Oscar Levant combined immense talent with an acerbic personality that made him a popular performer for decades. Originally from Pittsburgh, Levant moved to Hollywood, where he became friends with George Gershwin. By the 1940s, he was the highest-paid concert pianist in America. Levant became a household name as a regular on radio's *Information Please*, where his brilliance and cutting wit were put on display. He performed in such films as *Rhapsody in Blue* (1945), *An American in Paris* (1951), and *The Band Wagon* (1953). Levant's wife, June Gale, of the singing Gale Sisters, was the stepmother of screenwriter Nora Ephron, is buried outside in the lawn. Pictured above are Levant, Gale, and their three daughters.

ALAN LIVINGSTON (1917–2009), CORRIDOR OF MEMORIES. Capitol Records producer Alan Livingston created the character Bozo the Clown in 1946. Later, at NBC, Livingston created the television western *Bonanza*, for which his brother Jay (see page 20) wrote the theme song. Again with Capitol, Livingston famously blocked the release of the first Beatles singles in America, believing them to be unsuitable for this side of the Atlantic. Another of Livingston's lasting legacies is the circular Capitol Records building in Hollywood, which was designed to look like a stack of records on a turntable. Livingston was married to actress Nancy Olson, who appeared in *Sunset Boulevard* (1950) and *The Absent-Minded Professor* (1961). Above is a publicity shot of, from left to right, Pernell Roberts, Michael Landon, Dan Blocker, and Lorne Greene, the stars of *Bonanza*, one of Alan Livingston's most famous creations.

JAY LIVINGSTON (1915–2001), SANCTUARY OF PRAYER (PRIVATE UNDERGROUND VAULT); AND RAY EVANS (1915–2007), GARDENS OF SERENITY. The songwriting duo of composer Jay Livingston and lyricist Ray Evans met while students in the 1930s. They scored their first number-one hit with "To Each His Own" that same year. In 1947, their song "Buttons and Bows," from *The Paleface*, became a top-10 hit for four different performers and won the Academy Award for Best Song. They later won Oscars for "Mona Lisa" and "Que Sera Sera" and were nominated for another for "Tammy." The duo famously wrote the theme songs for *Bonanza* and *Mr. Ed* and the Christmas standard "Silver Bells." Livingston is buried with his actress wife, Shirley Mitchell, in the Underground Sanctuary of Prayer, which is off-limits to tourists. Evans is buried with his wife, actress Wyn Ritchie, in the Gardens of Serenity. In the photograph are, from left to right, Ray Evans, Jay Livingston, and three unidentified men.

ROBERT LOGGIA (1930–2015), SANCTUARY OF SERENITY. When Tom Hanks danced on the giant piano keyboard in *Big* (1989), as seen here, his duet partner on "Chopsticks" was none other than American actor Robert Loggia. Loggia had a career spanning more than six decades, appearing in several classic films and television shows. His acting career began at age 25 in his hometown of New York. Loggia would go on to appear in *An Officer and a Gentleman* (1982), *Scarface* (1983), *Prizzi's Honor* (1985), and *Independence Day* (1996). He was nominated for Best Supporting Actor in *Jagged Edge* in 1985. Although he was usually cast as a "heavy," in *Big*, Loggia proved he was equally adept in comedic roles.

DEAN MARTIN (1917–1995), SANCTUARY OF LOVE. Singer, actor, and comedian Dean Martin, a member of filmdom's Rat Pack, was one of the most enduring entertainers of the 20th century. Martin began his career partnered with comedian Jerry Lewis performing in nightclubs and successfully on screen and television for a decade. After the partnership dissolved, Martin continued singing and joking on screen with such stars as fellow Rat Packers Frank Sinatra and Sammy Davis Jr. in the original *Ocean's 11* (1960), in which Westwood neighbor Richard Conte made an appearance. He also starred in *Robin and the Seven Hoods* (1964), which featured Westwooder Peter Falk. He later played in westerns opposite John Wayne in *Rio Bravo* (1959) and *The Sons of Katie Elder* (1965).

DEAN MARTIN (1917–1995), SANCTUARY OF LOVE. Dean Martin recorded over 100 albums and had several million sellers including "Ain't That a Kick in the Head," written by Westwooder Sammy Cahn, and "Everybody Loves Somebody," which knocked The Beatles' "A Hard Day's Night" off of the number-one spot in 1964. The following year, Martin launched a comedy-variety show on NBC called *The Dean Martin Show*, which lasted a decade. Martin appeared regularly in Las Vegas for decades and continued performing until shortly before his diagnosis of lung cancer in 1993. He died two years later, on Christmas Day, 1995. On his crypt is the opening line of his signature song "Everybody Loves Somebody." Dean's second wife, Jeanne, is buried near Marilyn Monroe. His son-in-law was Carl Wilson of The Beach Boys, who is also buried at Westwood. Figure skater Dorothy Hamill and actress Olivia Hussey were once Martin's daughters-in-law. Martin is seen above during one of his many Vegas appearances.

MARILYN MONROE (1926–1962), CORRIDOR OF MEMORIES. Perhaps the most iconic star in Hollywood history, beautiful blonde bombshell Marilyn Monroe is arguably as famous today as she was before her death over 60 years ago. Projecting a powerful mixture of sexuality and vulnerability on screen, Monroe is one of Hollywood's most enduring icons. Born in Los Angeles as Norma Jeane Mortenson in 1926, young Marilyn spent most of her early years in foster homes, orphanages, and in the care of Grace Goddard and Ana Atchinson Lower, who are both buried near the cemetery office.

MARILYN MONROE (1926–1962), CORRIDOR OF MEMORIES. Marilyn Monroe began modeling as a teenager and famously posed nude for a calendar in 1949 that would later become the first *Playboy* centerfold. She became one of the most marketable stars in the 1950s, appearing in such hits as *All About Eve* (1950), *The Asphalt Jungle* (1950), *Gentlemen Prefer Blondes* (1953), *How to Marry a Millionaire* (1953), *The Seven Year Itch* (1955), *Bus Stop* (1956), and *The Prince and the Showgirl* (1957). In 1959, she made *Some Like It Hot* with Westwood neighbors Jack Lemmon and Billy Wilder.

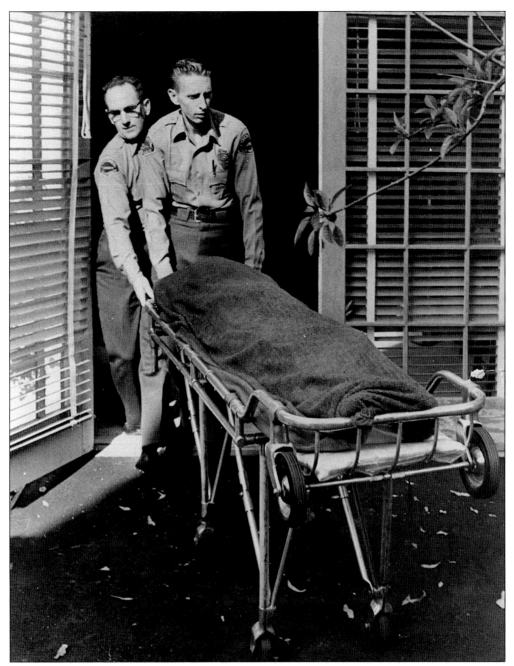

MARILYN MONROE (1926–1962), CORRIDOR OF MEMORIES. A troubled soul, Marilyn suffered for years from addiction and mood disorders. When she died in her home in Brentwood in August 1962 from a barbiturate overdose, it was ruled a suicide, but many have suspected foul play. Marilyn was married three times and reportedly had affairs with both Jack and Bobby Kennedy. Her marriage to Joe DiMaggio ended in divorce, but they remained close, and he arranged her funeral at Westwood. In the photograph above, two men wheel out the lifeless body of Marilyn Monroe from her home on August 5, 1962.

ROD MCKUEN (1933–2015), CORRIDOR OF MEMORIES. Poet, singer-songwriter, and composer Rod McKuen was one of the best-selling wordsmiths in American history, selling over 60 million copies of his books of poetry along with 100 million records. Born in 1933 into an abusive family in Oakland, McKuen ran away from home and supported himself with a wide array of low-paying jobs. Switching to poetry, he read in San Francisco clubs with Jack Kerouac and Allen Ginsburg. In the 1960s, McKuen moved to France where he translated the works of Belgian singer-songwriter Jacques Brel into English, which resulted in a few hits in America. McKuen wrote over 1,500 songs which were covered by numerous artists including Barbra Streisand, Johnny Cash, and Frank Sinatra. Moving to Hollywood, McKuen composed for films, earning two Academy Award nominations. Never a hit with critics or academics, McKuen once said that "the most unforgivable sin in the world is to be a bestselling poet."

WAITE PHILLIPS (1883–1964), PRIVATE MAUSOLEUM. Waite Phillips revolutionized the petroleum industry by creating a way to pump, refine, and distribute oil and gasoline at the beginning of America's conversion to automobile travel. Phillips Petroleum, which he created with his brothers, was nationally known for its Phillips 66 stations. Phillips sold his portion of the business and began developing office complexes such as the Philtower and Philcade buildings in Tulsa, Oklahoma. Phillips donated many of his properties to worthy causes, including his home in Tulsa, which became the Philbrook Museum of Art (seen above), and 127,000 acres of his New Mexico ranch property to the Boy Scouts of America.

RICHARD QUINE (1920–1989), ROOM OF PRAYER. Richard Quine's first acting role on film was 1941's *Babes on Broadway*, starring Judy Garland and Mickey Rooney. The following year, he appeared as Garland's brother in *For Me and My Gal*. He later transitioned to directing, with his most popular films being *The Solid Gold Cadillac* (1956), *Bell, Book and Candle* (1958), *The World of Suzie Wong* (1960), *Sex and the Single Girl* (1964), and *How to Murder Your Wife* (1965). Quine often cowrote scripts with Blake Edwards and was known for dating several famous actresses, including Judy Holliday, Kim Novak, and Westwood neighbor Natalie Wood.

WAYNE ROGERS (1933–2015), SANCTUARY OF SERENITY. Actor and financier Wayne Rogers's big break came at age 39 when he was cast as "Trapper John" on the television adaptation of the popular Korean War dark comedy M*A*S*H. He appeared in three seasons of the show before leaving over a contract dispute. His next starring role was in the three-season sitcom *House Calls*. Switching careers, Rogers began managing finances for other Hollywood stars. This led to appearances as an expert witness before Congress, where he advocated for sensible bank regulations. He also appeared regularly as a panelist on the Fox Business show *Cashin' In*.

LES TREMAYNE (1913–2003), SANCTUARY OF SERENITY. Actor Les Tremayne was born in London and moved with his family to Chicago at the age of four. He worked in radio as a teenager and starred in several popular programs, including *The First Nighter Program* and *Abbott Mysteries*. Switching to film, he appeared in *The War of the Worlds* (1953), *A Man Called Peter* (1955), *The Monster of Piedras Blancas* (1959), *North by Northwest* (1959), and *Angry Red Planet* (1959). His television credits include episodes of *Perry Mason*, *The Andy Griffith Show*, *My Favorite Martian*, and *General Hospital*.

ROBERT STACK (1919–2003), ROOM OF PRAYER. Robert Stack was a familiar face in Hollywood over a seven-decade career. He appeared in a few films before serving as an officer in the Navy during World War II. After the war, his films included *Fighter Squadron* (1948), *A Date with Judy* (1948), and *Bullfighter and the Lady* (1951). In the mid-1950s his career was boosted when he appeared with John Wayne in *The High and the Mighty* (1954) and the Douglas Sirk film *Written on the Wind* (1956), for which he was nominated for an Academy Award for Best Supporting Actor. In 1959, Stack was cast as Eliot Ness in the television show *The Untouchables*, for which he won the Best Actor Emmy. He continued making films and shows into the 1980s when he became known as a comedic actor in films including *Airplane!* (1980), *1941* (1979), and *Joe Versus the Volcano* (1990). In 1987, he began hosting *Unsolved Mysteries*, which continued through 2002, a year before his death. Below, Stack dines with Olivia de Havilland in an undated photograph.

JOSEF VON STERNBERG (1894–1969), SANCTUARY OF PRAYER. Silent and early talkie film director Josef Von Sternberg was born into an Orthodox Jewish family in Vienna. His tyrannical father abused his mother and limited his children's activities to only religious studies and schoolwork. He moved to New York when he was 14 and worked various jobs, including a position at the World Film Company in Fort Lee, New Jersey, where he became a projectionist and was later put in charge of writing titles and editing silent films. Von Sternberg worked with Mary Pickford before moving to MGM in 1925 and then to Paramount two years later. His magnum opus was *The Blue Angel* (1930) starring Marlene Dietrich, which launched a six-movie collaboration between the pair. The "von" in his name was added for "artistic prestige." Curiously, Von Sternberg has not one, but two gravesites in Westwood.

Two

SECTION 2

Section 2 stretches west from the Private Garden, which is off-limits to tourists, to the chapel. It encompasses the Rose Garden, several grassy private plots, and the Gardens of Serenity, a courtyard with lots of flowing fountains surrounded by rows of small crypts. This area, which is one of the priciest pieces of real estate in Los Angeles, contains the graves of many of the most famous people in history.

Among the luminaries found in this small area are Patty Andrews, Ray Bradbury, Fanny Brice, Les Brown, James Coburn, Rodney Dangerfield, Marvin Davis, Don DeFore, Kirk Douglas, Peter Falk, Farrah Fawcett, Merv Griffin, Florence Henderson, Jack Klugman, Peggy Lee, Janet Leigh Jack Lemmon, Mahasti, Walter Matthau, Karl Malden, Carroll O'Connor, Patti Page, Wolfgang Petersen, George C. Scott, Alvin Toffler, and Billy Wilder.

Some of the other residents may not be household names, but their creations are world-famous. Sam Simon, one of the creators of *The Simpsons*, is here in a grassy plot near one occupied by William J. and Lee Phillip Bell, who produced the soap operas *The Young and the Restless* and *The Bold and the Beautiful*. Bong Soo Han, the "Father of Hapkido" is here, as is producer John J. Carsey, who worked on shows like *The Tonight Show* and *Rowan & Martin's Laugh-In*. He was married for over 30 years to super-producer Marcy Carsey.

In the Rose Garden, look for the tiny memorials for Mary Carlisle, Connie Hines, Don DeFore, Jack Armstrong, and Stan Kenton. Also found here is the plaque for Bebe Goddard, who was a childhood friend of Marilyn Monroe and is memorialized as "Norma Jeane's Foster Sister."

PATTY ANDREWS (1918–2013), GARDENS OF SERENITY. In the columbarium is the small crypt of Patty Andrews, who, along with sisters Maxene and LaVerne, provided much of the soundtrack of the 1930s and 1940s. The Andrew Sisters struck gold 19 times in their career and sold over 75 million records. Their biggest hit came in 1941 with "The Boogie Woogie Bugle Boy of Company B." Originally from Minneapolis, the Andrews Sisters had their first hit with 1937's "Bei Mir Bist Du Schon," which was written by fellow Westwood resident Sammy Cahn. Above, from left to right, are Maxene, Patty, and LaVerne Andrews.

KEN ANNAKIN (1914–2009), GARDENS OF SERENITY. British film director Ken Annakin spent years doing documentaries and features in England before making the live-action film *The Story of Robin Hood* (1952) for Walt Disney. In 1960, he helmed another hit for Disney with *Swiss Family Robinson.* Two years later, Westwood neighbor Darryl F. Zanuck hired Annakin to direct *The Longest Day* followed by *Those Magnificent Men in Their Flying Machines* in 1965. Annakin also directed the war film *The Battle of the Bulge* that same year. In 2001, Annakin wrote his autobiography entitled *So You Wanna Be a Director?* Pictured is a scene from *The Story of Robin Hood* with Patrick Barr and Richard Todd.

32

ROBERT ARMSTRONG (1890–1973), ROSE
GARDEN. Actor Robert Armstrong is one
of several Westwood residents who are
famous for their work on the 1933 film *King
Kong*. After filming *Kong* during the day,
Armstrong and costar Fay Wray worked
at night for codirector Merian C. Cooper
in *The Most Dangerous Game*, which used
the same sets. Armstrong died in 1973,
within a day of Cooper. He stands third
from the right (with the light-colored
sleeve) in this still from *King Kong*.

JACK ARNOLD (1916–1992), ROSE GARDEN.
Director Jack Arnold specialized in science-
fiction and horror films during a career
that peaked in the 1950s. We have him
to thank for the enduring classics *It Came
From Outer Space* (1953); *Creature from the
Black Lagoon* (1954); *Tarantula!* (1955)—
which featured character actor Steve
Darrell, whose ashes were scattered in
the same area; and *The Incredible Shrinking
Man* (1957). A documentary of his life
entitled *The Incredible Thinking Man*, was
produced in 1992, the year of his death.

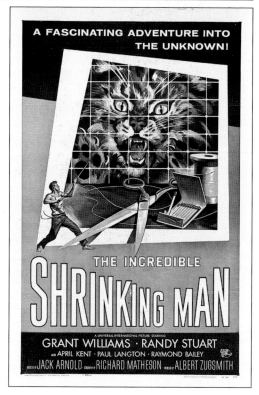

WILLIAM J. BELL (1927–2005) AND LEE PHILLIP BELL (1928–2020), GARDENS OF SERENITY. Daytime drama producer William Bell worked for decades as a writer and producer of *Another World*, *The Young and the Restless*, and *The Bold and the Beautiful*. He is buried with his wife, Lee Phillip Bell, who hosted over 10,000 episodes during a talk show career in Chicago. She also cocreated *The Young and the Restless* and *The Bold and the Beautiful* with her husband. Today, several of their children continue working in soap operas.

BILLY BLETCHER (1894–1979), ROSE GARDEN. Some of the residents of Westwood, like Billy Bletcher, had careers that started in the silent era. Lucky for us, films began talking, which spotlighted the talent of voice actors like Bletcher. His voice appeared in many of the classic animated shorts of Walt Disney, Warner Bros., and MGM. He also appeared in front of the camera in Laurel and Hardy's classic comedy *Babes In Toyland* (1934) and later provided the voice for the mayor of Munchkinland in *The Wizard of Oz* (1939).

RAY BRADBURY (1920–2012), GARDENS OF SERENITY. It is difficult to speak of the science-fiction genre without mentioning the name Ray Bradbury. Born in Illinois and raised in Los Angeles, Bradbury began writing science-fiction and fantasy stories for fanzines as a teenager in the late 1930s. He continued writing until his death and produced a prolific output of over 500 titles. Among his best-known books are *The Martian Chronicles* (1950), *Something Wicked This Way Comes* (1962), and *I Sing the Body Electric* (1969). His most famous work was 1953's *Fahrenheit 451*, which has been adapted for the screen many times. Bradbury was justifiably proud of this work as witnessed by the epitaph on his headstone which reads, "Author of Fahrenheit 451." Bernie Taupin, Elton John's lyricist, recently revealed that the idea for the hit song "Rocket Man" came from a Bradbury short story.

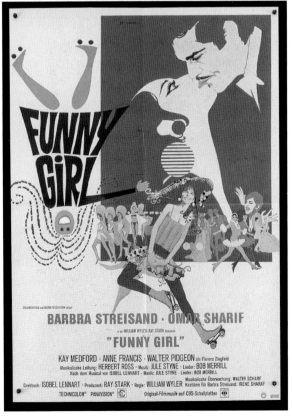

FANNY BRICE (1891–1951), GARDENS OF SERENITY. Comedienne Fanny Brice began her career as a singer on Broadway in the Ziegfeld Follies and made her big screen debut in 1928. A star on stage, screen, and radio, her career came full circle when she played her Follies-self on-screen in *The Great Ziegfeld* (1936), which won the Best Picture Oscar. Brice was reintroduced to a new audience over a decade after her death by Barbra Streisand, who won a Best Actress Oscar for playing her in *Funny Girl* (1968). Brice is interred near other members of her family, including her brother, actor Lew Brice, her son William, who was an accomplished painter, and son-in-law Ray Stark, who produced *Funny Girl* and several other films over a long career. Brice was originally interred in the Home of Peace Cemetery in Los Angeles.

LES BROWN (1912–2001), GARDENS OF SERENITY. American jazz bandleader Les Brown, along with his "Band of Renown," was a familiar presence on stage, screen, and television for nearly 70 years. Brown and his band scored 10 number-one hits, performed with nearly every famous singer of the era, and helped bring Doris Day to prominence. They performed with Bob Hope for nearly 50 years and appeared in several films, including *The Nutty Professor* (1963) with Jerry Lewis. They were also the house band for *The Steve Allen Show* and for Dean Martin, his Westwood neighbor, on *The Dean Martin Show*. Brown died in 2001 from lung cancer. His son Les Brown Jr. continued leading the Band of Renown until his passing in 2023.

VANESSA BROWN (1928–1999), ROSE GARDEN. Actress Vanessa Brown was born in Vienna to Jewish parents who fled the Nazis. Brown went on to star on stage, radio, and in film. She was fluent in several languages and reportedly had an IQ of 165. Brown put her brainpower on display for two years on the radio program *Quiz Kids*. In another of the many Westwood connections between Marilyn Monroe and other permanent residents of the cemetery, Brown originated the role of "The Girl" on stage in the Broadway production, *The Seven Year Itch*, a role that Marilyn played on screen in 1955.

MARY CARLISLE (1914–2018), ROSE GARDEN. Blonde-haired, blue-eyed beauty Mary Carlisle passed away in 2018 at the advanced age of 104. She was reportedly discovered in the Universal Studios commissary at the age of 14 and started her screen career in Cecil B. DeMille's *Madam Satan* (1930). Carlisle appeared in over 60 films spanning a 12-year career during Hollywood's Golden Age. Her most famous roles came in three Bing Crosby musical comedies in the 1930s.

GARRETT-HOWARD

JAMES COBURN (1928–2002), GARDENS OF SERENITY. Tall and toothy, actor James Coburn appeared in over 70 films and 100 episodes of television during a 45-year career. Coburn was often seen in Westerns and war films and became a star playing suave spy Derek Flint in a series of films for Fox. Coburn famously earned $250,000 per word for a beer commercial in the 1970s with the line "Schlitz Light." Coburn appeared on the cover of Paul McCartney and Wings' 1973 *Band on the Run* album (which was engineered by Westwood neighbor Geoff Emerick) and earned an Oscar for his work in *Affliction* (1997). He voiced the role of Henry J. Waternoose III in Pixar's *Monsters, Inc.* in 2001. A fan of fast cars and martial arts, Coburn was a good friend of Bruce Lee and served as one of his pallbearers. In 1972, Coburn starred in *The Honkers*, which was written and directed by Steve Ihnat, who is buried in a crypt near Marilyn Monroe.

RODNEY DANGERFIELD (1921–2004), GARDENS OF SERENITY. The aluminum siding industry lost a great salesman when Rodney Dangerfield took up comedy full-time at age 40. Born Jacob Rodney Cohen in 1921, Dangerfield went on to have a legendary career as a standup comic and actor, appearing in such noted films as *Caddyshack* (1980), *Easy Money* (1983), and *Back to School* (1986).

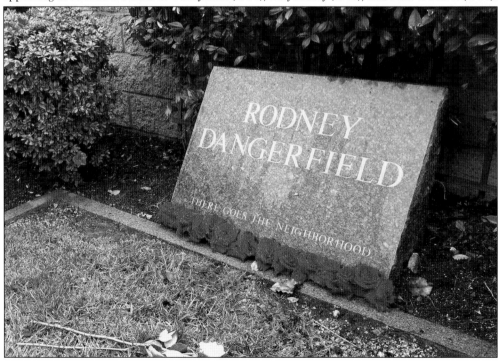

RODNEY DANGERFIELD (1921–2004), GARDENS OF SERENITY. Rodney Dangerfield opened a comedy club in New York called Dangerfield's, which helped launch the careers of comedians Jim Carrey, Roseanne Barr, Tim Allen, and Sam Kinison. The man famous for his line "I Don't Get No Respect!" carried his self-deprecating humor into the afterlife, as his headstone reads, "There Goes the Neighborhood."

MARVIN DAVIS (1925–2004), GARDENS OF SERENITY. Oilman Marvin Davis became a Hollywood mogul when he used the money he made as a wildcatter to purchase the 20th Century Fox studio in 1981, which he later sold to Rupert Murdoch. Davis also used some of his $6 billion fortune to purchase the Beverly Hills Hotel and made extensive investments in resorts in Pebble Beach and Aspen. The Carrington family on the TV show *Dynasty* was said to be loosely based on Davis and his family. Davis's grandson Jason, a voice actor who died of a fentanyl overdose in 2020 at the age of 35, is buried nearby. Davis is seen here with his wife of 53 years, Barbara Levine.

DON DEFORE (1913–1993), ROSE GARDEN. Actor Don DeFore enjoyed a long television and film career. He is best remembered for his work on *The Adventures of Ozzie and Harriet* (alongside Westwooder David Nelson) and later as the costar of *Hazel*, opposite Shirley Booth. For several years, DeFore and his family operated a restaurant at Disneyland. He also served as the honorary mayor of the village of Brentwood, which is a few miles west of the cemetery.

KIRK DOUGLAS (1916–2020), GARDENS OF SERENITY. Issur Danielovitch was born in New York to Russian-Jewish immigrant parents and grew up as their only son along with six sisters. He left his name and an impoverished adolescence behind and resurfaced as the iconic American leading man Kirk Douglas. After sustaining an injury in World War II, Douglas pursued acting in New York, helped in his career by his classmate Lauren Bacall. Moving to Hollywood, Douglas earned his first Best Actor nomination for *Champion* (1949). He got his second three years later for *The Bad and the Beautiful* and a third for *Lust For Life* (1956).

KIRK DOUGLAS (1916–2020), GARDENS OF SERENITY. Like his friend and Westwood neighbor Burt Lancaster, Douglas began producing the films he starred in, like the classics *Paths of Glory* (1957) and *Spartacus* (1960), which brought fame to newcomer director Stanley Kubrick. He also purchased the rights to the play *One Flew Over the Cuckoo's Nest* for his actor-producer son Michael, who turned it into the Best Picture of 1975. Douglas received an honorary Oscar and was awarded a Presidential Medal of Freedom. He and Anne Buydens, his wife of over 60 years, were well known for their philanthropy. Douglas died at the age of 103, and his wife lived to be 102. They are buried with their son Eric, who died of a drug overdose. Here, Douglas is seen in a still from *Spartacus*.

PETER FALK (1927–2011), GARDENS OF SERENITY. Peter Falk was a familiar presence on screen and television during a very long Hollywood career. Frequently featured in big-budget comedies, Falk is best known for his starring role as the rumpled, yet deceptively brilliant murder investigator Lieutenant Columbo, in the series *Columbo*. He is also known for his work with director and Westwood neighbor John Cassavetes and for being nominated twice for Oscars and Emmys during the same year. Falk lost an eye to cancer at the age of three and wore a glass eye for the remainder of his life. Falk's second marriage was to actress Shera Danese, who often guest-starred on *Columbo*. His epitaph reads, "I'm not here. I'm home with Shera."

FARRAH FAWCETT (1947–2009), GARDENS OF SERENITY. Texan actress and model Farrah Fawcett became an international sensation in the 1970s playing Jill Munroe in the first season of *Charlie's Angels*. After being named one of the "ten most beautiful coeds on campus" at the University of Texas, she secured a Hollywood agent and moved to Southern California. For several years, she appeared in commercials and made guest appearances on television shows before posing in 1976 in a red bathing suit that became the best-selling poster in history. This led to her role in *Charlie's Angels*. After only one season, Fawcett moved on to more serious roles in films like *The Burning Bed* (1974) and *Small Sacrifices* (1989), which both earned her Emmy nominations. Her grave, in the Gardens of Serenity, is just to the right of Merv Griffin's plot.

FARRAH FAWCETT (1947–2009), GARDENS OF SERENITY. Farrah Fawcett was once married to actor Lee Majors and was in a long-term relationship with actor Ryan O'Neal. Fawcett was diagnosed with cancer in 2006 and filmed her battle with the disease in the documentary, *Farrah's Story.* She succumbed at the age of 62 on June 25, 2009, which was overshadowed in the media when megastar Michael Jackson coincidentally died of a drug overdose on the same day. While married to Majors, a conversation between Fawcett and songwriter Jim Weatherly was the inspiration for the song "Midnight Train to Georgia," which topped the charts for Gladys Knight & the Pips in 1973. Fawcett posed twice for Westwood neighbor Hugh Hefner's *Playboy* magazine in the mid-1990s. Seen here are Ryan O'Neal and Fawcett in this undated photograph.

CHUCK FRIES (1928–2021), GARDENS OF SERENITY. Chuck Fries, the founder of Fries Entertainment, was a producer of movies and television mini-series, including *The Martian Chronicles* in 1980, based on the Ray Bradbury novel. He also produced the film *Future Shock* (1972), which was based on Alvin Toffler's non-fiction book of the same name. In 1989, Fries made *Small Sacrifices*, starring Farrah Fawcett. Today, Fries, Bradbury, Toffler, and Fawcett are all buried within steps of one another. (Photograph by E.J. Stephens.)

JANE GREER (1924–2001), GARDENS OF SERENITY. Actress Jane Greer enjoyed a long career in film and television. Born in Washington, DC, as a teenager she suffered from facial palsy, which paralyzed the left side of her face and gave her an expression that RKO would later use to promote her as "The Woman with the Mona Lisa Smile." Greer acted in several movies during the 1940s, most notably in the film noir classic *Out of the Past* (1947) with Westwood neighbor Kirk Douglas. In the 1970s, Greer appeared on *Quincy, M.E.* with Jack Klugman and on an episode of *Columbo*, starring Peter Falk. Both men are now buried just steps away from her crypt.

Merv Griffin (1925–2007), Gardens of Serenity. Talk show host and producer Merv Griffin turned his childhood love of the game Hangman into the wildly successful game show, *Wheel of Fortune*. Griffin first made a name for himself as a big band singer and radio host. In 1950, he had a number-one hit with "I've Got a Lovely Bunch of Coconuts." Griffin appeared in a few musicals for Warner Bros. before turning his attention to television. He was soon hosting his own talk show and producing game shows, creating *Jeopardy!* in 1964 and *Wheel of Fortune* 11 years later. In 1986, Griffin sold his production company to Columbia Pictures for $250 million. He also made several fortunes buying and selling hotels and resorts. At the time of his death, his net worth was north of $1 billion. Griffin once stated that his epitaph would be "Stay Tuned." Instead, his headstone reads "I will not be right back after this message." His best friend, Eva Gabor, is also buried in Westwood. Griffin, third from the left, is pictured with Alex Trebec, the longtime host of *Jeopardy!*, along with Vanna White and Pat Sajak of *Wheel of Fortune*.

49

FLORENCE HENDERSON (1934–2016), GARDENS OF SERENITY. Actress Florence Henderson was born in Southern Indiana in 1934. The youngest of 10 children, Henderson began her career on stage. In 1962, she became the first woman to guest host *The Tonight Show*. Henderson became a household name playing Carol Brady in television's *The Brady Bunch* during the 1970s. Allan Melvin, who played Sam the Butcher in the show, is buried nearby. Henderson's second marriage was to a hypnotherapist who treated her for depression and stage fright in the early 1980s. They remained together until his death in 2002. Henderson died of heart failure in 2016 at age 82.

BRIAN KEITH (1921–1997), GARDENS OF SERENITY. Actor Brian Keith had a six-decade career as a leading man on stage, film, and television. On screen he was most famous for his roles in *The Parent Trap* (1961) and *The Wind and the Lion* (1975). He was also a familiar face on television playing the starring roles on *Family Affair*, with Westwooder Sebastian Cabot, and later on *Hardcastle and McCormick*. Keith died of a self-inflicted gunshot wound at age 75 in 1997. His death came just two months after the suicide of his daughter Daisy. Today, they are interred together. (Photograph by E.J. Stephens.)

NANCY KELLY (1921–1995), ROSE GARDEN. Nancy Kelly was a child actress in the late 1920s, who became a leading lady during the 1930s and 1940s. In the late 1940s, Kelly acted regularly on stage, most notably as the mother in *The Bad Seed* (1956). She revived the role on screen in 1956 and earned a Best Actress nomination. Kelly was married for a time to actor Edmond O'Brien. She was the older sister of actor Jack Kelly Jr., who was a regular on TV's *Maverick* and later served as the mayor of Huntington Beach, California. Above, she is pictured on the right with Patty McCormick in the film version of *The Bad Seed*.

STAN KENTON (1911–1979), ROSE GARDEN. Innovative jazz pianist Stan Kenton was a bandleader for over 40 years, working with many of the greatest jazz performers of the day. He was taught the piano by his mother and performed with several bands during high school. He formed his own band in 1941 and had a hit two years later with "Artistry In Rhythm." In the late 1940s, Kenton debuted a more experimental sound, alienating some jazz purists. Kenton kept performing until the mid-1970s. His second marriage (of three) to singer Anne Richards ended after she appeared nude in Westwood neighbor Hugh Hefner's *Playboy* magazine in June 1961, without his knowledge.

Victor Kilian (1891–1979) and Charles Wagenheim (1896–1979), Rose Garden. Character actor Victor Kilian gave a lot to Hollywood. In 1942, while practicing for a fight scene with John Wayne, he lost an eye. Later, during the McCarthy era, he was blacklisted because of his political beliefs, which cost him his livelihood. Kilian achieved his greatest success in 1976 playing the "Fernwood Flasher" on the series *Mary Hartman, Mary Hartman*. Three years later, Kilian was living in an apartment in Hollywood when he was beaten to death by burglars. In a bizarre series of coincidences, veteran character actor Charles Wagenheim had been beaten to death only five days earlier in his apartment, just two miles away from where Kilian was killed. (The day Wagenheim was killed happened to be Kilian's birthday.) Both Kilian and Wagenheim appeared in the same episode of *All in the Family*, starring Westwood neighbor Carroll O'Connor, that was broadcast just days after their murders. Both Kilian and Wagenheim were cremated and had their ashes scattered in Westwood's Rose Garden. Some psychics claim that Kilian's ghost wanders the forecourt of the TCL Chinese Theatre in Hollywood, pictured above.

JACK KLUGMAN (1922–2012), GARDENS OF SERENITY. When Jack Klugman was in college, his drama teacher thought so little of his talent that he recommended that Klugman become a truck driver. Luckily, he did not take this advice. Klugman's career on television began in the 1950s and peaked in the 1970s when he won Emmys for starring in two popular series: *The Odd Couple*, costarring Tony Randall, and *Quincy, M.E.*, where he played a forensic pathologist. Klugman and Randall remained close for the remainder of their lives. In 2005, Klugman published a book entitled *Tony and Me: A Story of Friendship*, which came out a year after Randall's passing. Klugman died of cancer in 2012 at age 90. His small crypt sits next to Janet Leigh (see page 55), another Hollywood legend.

PEGGY LEE (1920–2002), GARDENS OF SERENITY. Born Norma Egstrom into a Scandinavian-American home in 1920, Peggy Lee, the "Queen of American pop music," began her singing career on a North Dakota radio station. Migrating as a teenager to Southern California, she got a job with bandleader Benny Goodman. Lee had her first hit in 1942 and followed up with the million-selling "Why Don't You Do Right?" the following year. Even though it was against policy for her to fraternize with the band members, Lee married Dave Barbour, the band's guitarist, which got them both fired. Lee and Barbour began writing songs together, which produced several hits, including "Mañana" in 1947. She appeared on several popular radio shows during the late 1940s and 1950s and had a huge hit with "Fever" in 1958. Lee was also a success on screen earning a Best Supporting Actress nomination for *Pete Kelly's Blues* (1958). She was a frequent guest on television shows for decades and provided several voices for Disney's animated classic, *Lady and the Tramp* (1955). Lee died at age 81 in 2002. Barbour, her first husband and writing partner, is buried with her.

JANET LEIGH (1927–2004), GARDENS OF SERENITY. Janet Leigh's performance in *Psycho* made people fear taking a shower for decades. Born in Central California in 1927, Jeanette Helen Morrison was discovered at age 18 by actress Norma Shearer, who helped her land a contract at MGM. Leigh appeared in a series of films in the 1950s, including the film noir masterpiece *Touch of Evil* (1958). Two years later, she appeared as Marion Crane in Alfred Hitchcock's horror classic, *Psycho* (1960), for which she was nominated for an Oscar. Crane's murder by Norman Bates while she is showering terrorized thousands of viewers; apparently even Leigh herself, who reportedly only took baths for years afterward. Leigh also starred in *The Manchurian Candidate* in 1962, the year she divorced actor Tony Curtis, when their daughter, future actress Jamie Leigh Curtis, was five. Leigh died in 2004 at the age of 77.

JACK LEMMON (1925–2001), GARDENS OF SERENITY. Everyman actor Jack Lemmon was equally adept in dramas and comedies in the 60 films he starred in over a long Hollywood career. Lemmon was nominated for Academy Awards a phenomenal eight times, winning twice. A sickly child, he began his acting career while attending Harvard. Lemmon was a talented musician and worked for a time as a piano player in New York bars. In Hollywood, his first leading role came in the Judy Holliday comedy *It Should Happen to You* (1954). This led to *Mister Roberts* (1955, for which he won the Best Supporting Actor Oscar), *Some Like It Hot* (1959, with several members of the Westwood family), *The Apartment* (1960), and *The Great Race* (1965).

JACK LEMMON (1925–2001), GARDENS OF SERENITY. Jack Lemmon frequently costarred with Walter Matthau (who is buried just steps away from him) during the next several years, most notably in *The Fortune Cookie* (1966), *The Odd Couple* (1968, seen above), and *Grumpy Old Men* (1993). Lemmon won the Best Actor Oscar in 1973 for *Save the Tiger*. He and his second wife, Felicia Farr, were married in 1962 and remained together until the end of his life. Lemmon was originally interred in a crypt on the opposite side of the cemetery before being reburied in his current location.

City of Los Angeles
State of California

Certificate of Tribute
is hereby presented to

Hayedeh

(Posthumously)

The City of Los Angeles proudly recognizes and remembers Ma'soumeh Dadahbala, also known as Hayedeh for her profound artistic contributions to the Iranian community as one of the most outstanding soprano singers of all time. The generous love and unending accolades from her nation transcended her to become a national icon and diva. During the Islamic revolution of 1979, she was forced to flee her beloved home country, and relocated to the United States where she dedicated her life to the Iranian American community in the City of Los Angeles. She spent her days in the heart of Tehrangeles in Westwood. Hayedeh's albums are still best sellers and her songs are ageless songs that have carried on her legacy. Hayedeh was graceful, uniquely talented, and shared with all her passion and love. We join in celebrating her life along with all who knew and loved her.

April 5, 2019

PAUL KORETZ
Councilmember 5th District

MAHASTI (1946–2007), GARDENS OF SERENITY, AND HAYEDEH (1942–1990), SECTION 4. Iranian singer Eftekhar Dadahbala, who performed under the name Mahasti, had a long career singing Persian classical, folk, and pop music from 1965 until her death. Mahasti's classy persona cleared a path for other female Iranian singers to prosper, including her sister Hayedeh, who was five years older. Hayedeh, like Mahasti, became one of the most popular and influential Iranian singers in history. The sisters left Iran before the Islamic Revolution and settled in the "Tehrangeles" area of Los Angeles. Hayedeh died of a heart attack at age 47 in 1990 and Mahasti in 2007. Today, both sisters are interred in Westwood. Mahasti is in the Gardens of Serenity, and Hayedeh is buried about 100 feet to the north in Section 4. (Photograph by E.J. Stephens.)

KARL MALDEN (1912–2009), GARDENS OF SERENITY. American actor Karl Malden was a popular presence in film and television during a 60-year Hollywood career. Malden grew up speaking Serbian in Gary, Indiana, where his father worked in the steel mills. He changed his name from Mladen Sekulovich at the urging of director Elia Kazan when he was 22. For the remainder of his career, Malden would try to insert "Mladen Sekulovich" into his dialogue in each film. After a stint in World War II, Malden acted on stage until the early 1950s when his film career took off. In 1951, he won the Academy Award for Best Supporting Actor in Kazan's *A Streetcar Named Desire*. In 1953, Malden appeared in Alfred Hitchcock's *I Confess*. The following year, he costarred in *On the Waterfront* and earned another Oscar nomination.

KARL MALDEN (1912–2009), GARDENS OF SERENITY. During the 1960s, Karl Malden appeared in such notable films as *Pollyanna* (1960), *One-Eyed Jacks* (1961), *Birdman of Alcatraz* (1962) (starring Westwooder Burt Lancaster), *Gypsy* (1962), *How the West Was Won* (1962), and *The Cincinnati Kid* (1965). In 1970, Malden played one of his most memorable roles as Gen. Omar Bradley in *Patton* alongside Westwood neighbor George C. Scott. For five years, Malden was a familiar face on television as Lt. Mike Stone on *The Streets of San Francisco*, with Michael Douglas. Malden is buried near Michael's dad, Kirk. Malden's final acting role came in an episode of *The West Wing* in 2000. Malden is buried with his wife, Mona. They were married for over 70 years. Pictured above is a still from *The Streets of San Francisco* with Michael Douglas (left) and Malden.

WALTER MATTHAU (1920–2000), GARDENS OF SERENITY. Loveable curmudgeon Walter Matthau appeared on screen in dozens of classics over a 50-year Hollywood career. He is best remembered for his costarring roles with Westwood neighbor Jack Lemmon in 10 films, including *The Fortune Cookie* (1966, directed by Westwooder Billy Wilder, for which Matthau won the Best Supporting Actor Oscar), *The Odd Couple* (1968, pictured above), *The Front Page* (1974), and *Grumpy Old Men* (1993). His collaborations with Jack Lemmon created one of the most lasting friendships in Hollywood. He also starred on his own in *A Face in the Crowd* (1957), *King Creole* (1958), *Charade* (1963), *Hello, Dolly!* (1969), *The Sunshine Boys* (1975), and *The Bad News Bears* (1976).

WALTER MATTHAU (1920–2000), GARDENS OF SERENITY. Walter Matthau, the child of Jewish Eastern European immigrants, began acting after serving in World War II. His motion picture debut came in *The Kentuckian* (1955), with Westwooder Burt Lancaster. Another of his early roles was in *Lonely Are the Brave* (1962), with Westwood neighbor Kirk Douglas. Matthau battled poor health for years, finally succumbing to heart disease in 2000. His wife, Carol Marcus, who was married twice to writer William Saroyan, died three years later and is interred with him.

ROBERT NATHAN (1894–1985), GARDENS OF SERENITY. Celebrated American novelist and poet Robert Nathan wrote the novel *The Bishop's Wife*, which was later adapted into a film starring Cary Grant. His 1940 fantasy novel *Portrait of Jennie* was his biggest success and was turned into a film featuring Joseph Cotton and Jennifer Jones. Nathan attended Harvard University where he was the editor of the *Harvard Monthly* and was a classmate of E.E. Cummings. He continued working into the 1970s, writing novels, screenplays, teleplays, and poems.

DAVID NELSON (1936–2011), GARDENS OF SERENITY. The eldest son of Ozzie and Harriet Nelson and brother of Ricky Nelson, David Nelson gained fame portraying a fictional version of himself on the long-running 1950s and 1960s television hit *The Adventures of Ozzie and Harriet*. His work on the show led to a career directing in television and films. He continued to act as well, appearing on television in *Peyton Place* and on-screen in *Hondo* (1953) and *The Big Circus* (1959), for which he received positive reviews for playing a disturbed young man. His final role was in the John Waters film *Cry Baby* in 1990.

CARROLL O'CONNOR (1924–2001), GARDENS OF SERENITY. Carroll O'Connor is best remembered for his iconic role as Archie Bunker in television's *All in the Family* and its sequel *Archie Bunker's Place*. For his portrayal of this blue-collar, outspoken, often-bigoted character over 12 years and two series, he received four Emmy Awards. Beginning in the late 1980s, O'Connor starred in the television drama *In the Heat of the Night*. In the late 1990s, he played Helen Hunt's father in the situation comedy *Mad About You*. O'Connor is pictured above with Jean Stapleton in a scene from *All in the Family*.

CARROLL O'CONNOR (1924–2001), GARDENS OF SERENITY. In addition to his television work, Carroll O'Connor appeared in numerous popular films, including *Lonely Are the Brave* (1962), *Cleopatra* (1963), *Point Blank* (1967), and *Kelly's Heroes* (1970). O'Connor has the distinction of being the only male performer to have received Lead Actor Emmy Awards for both comedy and drama series. O'Connor is buried with his adopted son, actor Hugh O'Connor, who struggled with addiction for most of his adult life after beating cancer in his late teens. Hugh's death by suicide led to his father becoming an advocate for drug addiction treatment.

WOLFGANG PETERSEN (1941–2022). Wolfgang Petersen was a German screenwriter and director who rose to worldwide fame in 1981 with his celebrated World War II submarine film *Das Boot*. The film received six Academy Award nominations, including two for Petersen as writer and director. He followed up this success with the popular family film *The NeverEnding Story* in 1984. In the 1990s and early 2000s, Petersen made a string of successful action thrillers including *In the Line of Fire* (1993), *Outbreak* (1995), *Air Force One* (1997), *The Perfect Storm* (2000), *Troy* (2004), and *Poseidon* (2006). He returned to Germany in 2016 to make his final film, *Vier Gegen die Bank*. Petersen is pictured above on the set of *Poseidon*.

DORIS ROBERTS (1925–2016), GARDENS OF SERENITY. Actress Doris Roberts spent 20 years performing on New York stages and television productions before making her film debut in 1961. For decades she appeared in character roles in television shows and films, including *The Naked City*, *The Defenders*, *Mary Hartman, Mary Hartman*, *Soap*, *The Honeymoon Killers* (1970), *Little Murders* (1971), and *Rabbit Test* (1978). In the 1980s and 1990s, Roberts starred on television in *Remington Steele* and played Chevy Chase's mother-in-law in *National Lampoon's Christmas Vacation* (1989). She is best remembered today for playing Ray Romano's mother in the popular sitcom *Everybody Loves Raymond*, for which she was nominated seven times for Emmys, winning four.

GEORGE C. SCOTT (1927–1999), GARDENS OF SERENITY. George C. Scott accomplished a great many things during a long movie career, but one of the things he is best remembered for is what he *didn't* do in Hollywood. Scott made his film debut in *The Hanging Tree* in 1959 and earned his first Academy Award nomination for Best Supporting Actor in *Anatomy of a Murder* later that same year. He continued to work on stage, film, and television, with some of his most popular film roles being *The Hustler* (1961), *Dr. Strangelove* (1964), *The Bible: In the Beginning* (1966), *Exorcist III* (1990), and *The Rescuers Down Under* (1990). But it's for 1970's Best Picture winner *Patton*, for which Scott won the Best Actor award, that he is often remembered. Actually, it's for what happened *after* he won the Oscar that he is most remembered, when he famously refused to accept it.

GEORGE C. SCOTT (1927–1999), GARDENS OF SERENITY. George C. Scott was born in the tiny town of Wise, Virginia. After his mother passed away when Scott was only eight years old, he was raised by his father, who was an automobile executive. After graduating from high school, Scott joined the Marine Corps, where he served as an honor guard for military funerals at Arlington National Cemetery. He initially wanted to be a novelist before turning to drama while enrolled at the University of Missouri. Scott was married five times, twice to actress Colleen Dewhurst. His grave at Westwood, which is next to Walter Matthau's, is unmarked.

RAY STARK (1915–2004), GARDENS OF SERENITY. Ray Stark was a producer whose films from the 1960s through the 1980s were some of the most popular of the time. He cofounded Seven Arts Productions with Eliot Hyman in 1957, and some of their early successes included *Anatomy of a Murder* (1959), *The World of Suzie Wong* (1960), *West Side Story* (1961), and *Night of the Iguana* (1964). Stark left Seven Arts in 1966 and formed Rastar Productions, where the first film he produced was the hugely successful *Funny Girl* (1968). This launched the career of Barbra Streisand, who played Stark's mother-in-law in the film, Fanny Brice. Some of the other notable Rastar films include *The Owl and the Pussycat* (1970), *The Way We Were* (1973), *The Goodbye Girl* (1977), *Seems Like Old Times* (1980), and *Steel Magnolias* (1989). During his career, he had lasting partnerships with numerous stars and filmmakers like Barbra Streisand, Neil Simon, John Huston, and Westwood's Herbert Ross. In 1980, Stark received the Irving G. Thalberg Memorial Award from the Academy of Motion Picture Arts and Sciences for his body of work. In this undated photograph, from left to right are Stark, an unidentified man, Kirk Douglas, and Oleg Cassini.

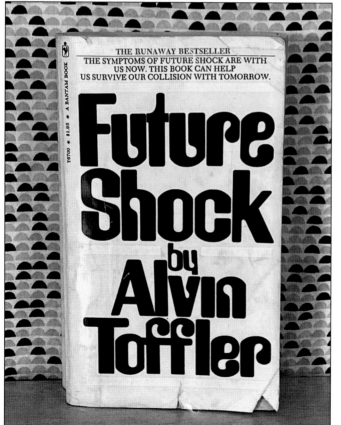

ALVIN TOFFLER (1928–2016), GARDENS OF SERENITY. Futurist Alvin Toffler was known for his books *Future Shock* (1970), *The Third Wave* (1980), and *Powershift* (1990). Among the trends he foresaw were the digital and communication revolutions, the rise of the personal computer, the internet, cable TV, mobile communication, and the effects of "information overload"—a term he coined—on cultures worldwide. Toffler is interred with his wife, Heidi, who collaborated on his books.

BILLY WILDER (1906–2002) AND AUDREY YOUNG (1922–2012), GARDENS OF SERENITY. Billy Wilder is regarded as one of the most brilliant writers and filmmakers in the history of cinema. He began his screenwriting career in Berlin, where he lived until immigrating to France after the rise of the Nazi Party in Germany. In 1934, he moved to Hollywood and began writing in the film noir style. He received Oscar nods for the romantic comedy *Ninotchka* (1939) and *Double Indemnity* (1944), becoming a household name to lovers of cinema.

BILLY WILDER (1906–2002) AND AUDREY YOUNG (1922–2012), GARDENS OF SERENITY. In 1949, Billy Wilder married talented singer Audrey Young, who is interred with him. The year 1957 was a memorable one for Wilder, with the success of *The Spirit of St. Louis, Love in the Afternoon,* and *Witness for the Prosecution,* for which he received a Best Director nomination. Wilder was also honored with the AFI Lifetime Achievement Award, the Producers Guild of America's Lifetime Achievement Award, the National Film Registry of the Library of Congress, and the BAFTA Fellowship Award. In this c. 1959 image are, from left to right, Walter Matthau, Wilder, and Jack Lemmon, who today are buried within steps of one another at Westwood.

Three

SECTION 3

Westwood Cemetery consists mostly of a large grassy field at the center of the burial ground surrounded by outdoor mausoleums and crypts. To make it easier to find people buried in this large plot, this field has been divided into two roughly equal portions, which, for this book, are called Sections 3 and 4.

To locate these sections, stand near the sidewalk at the east end of the chapel, with the Rose Garden to your left. Cross the road to the two black markers written in Farsi script, and look ahead toward the large tree. This line is used to demarcate the large plot, with Section 3 to the left and Section 4 to the right.

Section 3 contains the burial spots of such notables as Cornel Wilde, Natalie Wood, Donna Reed, Darryl F. Zanuck and his wife Virginia, Jim and Hennie Backus, Lew Ayres, Dominique Dunne, Richard Basehart, Nader Naderpour, Eddie and Margo Albert, Gregor Piatigorsky, Sammy Cahn, and the unmarked graves of Roy Orbison and Frank Zappa. In the southwest corner of the section is a large Urn Garden consisting of small square brown plaques. Among them are the graves of Milton Ager, Sebastian Cabot, and filmmakers Ernest and Ruth Rose Schoedsack. Close to the curb in this area are the graves of Grace Goddard and Ana Atchinson Lower, who took care of Marilyn Monroe when she was a girl.

MILTON AGER (1893–1979), URN GARDEN. One learns quickly at Westwood Cemetery that the size of a person's marker is in no way reflective of their accomplishments in life. A perfect example is found in the upper-right corner of the urn garden, across from the cemetery office. It is here that Milton Ager rests beneath one of the hundreds of lookalike foot-square brown markers. A member of the Songwriters Hall of Fame, Ager wrote such classics as "Chasing Rainbows," "Ain't She Sweet," and "Happy Days Are Here Again." Ager is interred near his daughter, journalist Shana Alexander (below), who became famous in the 1970s for her "Point-Counterpoint" segments on *60 Minutes* with James J. Kirkpatrick. (Photograph by Phil Lantis.)

EDDIE ALBERT (1906–2005) AND MARGO ALBERT (1917–1985). Even though he had a show biz career that landed him in such notable films as *Roman Holiday* (1953), *Oklahoma!* (1955), and *Teahouse of the August Moon* (1956), to millions of fans, Eddie Albert will forever be Oliver Wendell Douglas, the big city lawyer-turned-farmer on television's *Green Acres*. He is interred with his wife, Margo, an actress and dancer, who appeared in the film *Lost Horizon* in 1937. Their graves are less than 100 yards to the south of the burial plot of Eva Gabor, Eddie's costar on *Green Acres*. Gabor, first row at the far left, sits next to Albert in this publicity photo of the *Green Acres* cast.

LEW AYRES (1908–1996). Actor Lew Ayres made his big screen debut in 1929 and reached stardom the following year when he played the lead soldier in the antiwar classic *All Quiet on the Western Front* (pictured at right), which took home the Best Picture Oscar. A decade later, he appeared in eight *Young Dr. Kildare* films for MGM. His career was derailed at the start of World War II when he chose to be a conscientious objector, refusing to fight in combat. He still served overseas during the war as a medic, and his career revived after hostilities ended.

JIM BACKUS (1913–1989). Jim Backus's face and voice were seemingly everywhere on television during the 1950s and 1960s. He played millionaire Thurston Howell III on *Gilligan's Island* while also voicing the cartoon character *Mr. Magoo*, which lasted from 1949 until the late 1970s. Backus first gained attention on screen playing James Dean's father in *Rebel Without a Cause* in 1955. Backus is buried with his wife, Henny (pictured above), who was an actress and dancer. Together, they penned several best-selling comedy books.

RICHARD BASEHART (1914–1984). Ohio native Richard Basehart will long be remembered for his role as Admiral Harriman Nelson in television's *Voyage to the Bottom of the Sea.* During a lengthy acting career, Basehart often found himself performing near water. He starred as George S. Healey in *Titanic* (1953) and played Ishmael in *Moby Dick* (1956). Basehart rests under a small brown plaque that reads, "His Like Shall Never Come Again."

SEBASTIAN CABOT (1918–1977), URN GARDEN. Portly English character actor Sebastian Cabot first appeared on screen in Alfred Hitchcock's *Secret Agent* in 1936. He is best remembered for his role as Mr. French on the television show *Family Affair* (which starred Westwood neighbor Brian Keith). He also enjoyed a long career as a voice actor for Disney playing such notable roles as Bagheera in *Jungle Book* (1967) and the narrator of several *Winnie the Pooh* films. Cabot died in Canada at age 59.

SAMMY CAHN (1913–1993). It rarely snows in Southern California, but that never stopped songwriter Sammy Cahn from crafting the lyrics to one of the most enduring anthems of winter with "Let It Snow! Let It Snow! Let It Snow!" Cahn grew up playing the violin on New York's Lower East Side. This led to employment as a songwriter with Warner Bros. for their early Vitagraph shorts, and cowriting songs for a variety of performers, including Frank Sinatra. Cahn composed the lyrics to one of Sinatra's signature songs, "Love and Marriage," which gained a whole new audience decades after it was written when it was used as the theme song for television's *Married . . . With Children.* Cahn was nominated for an astounding 31 Oscars, winning four times for "Three Coins in the Fountain" (1954), "All the Way" (1957), "High Hopes" (1959), and "Call Me Irresponsible" (1963). He also wrote such memorable songs as "Ain't Love a Kick in the Head?" for Westwooder Dean Martin, "My Kind of Town," "Come Fly With Me," and "You Can Fly, You Can Fly, You Can Fly!" for Disney's animated classic *Peter Pan.* Cahn died in 1993 at age 79.

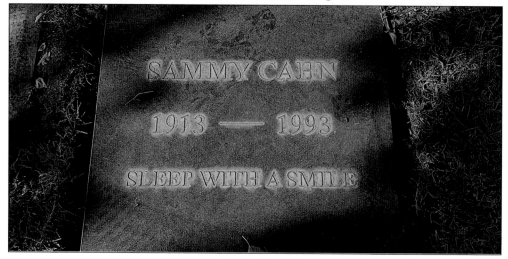

RICHARD DAWSON (1932–2012). British-born comic Richard Dawson is remembered for his roles as Corporal Newkirk on *Hogan's Heroes* (alongside Westwood neighbors Bob Crane and Sigrid Valdis) and later as the host of the game show *Family Feud*. Born Colin Emm in Gosport, England, Dawson was famous (perhaps infamous) for kissing all the *Feud's* female contestants on the lips. He was married twice, first to British sex symbol Diana Dors and later to one of the hundreds of women he kissed on *Family Feud*.

DOMINIQUE DUNNE (1959–1982). Actress Dominique Dunne was still appearing on screens across America in the supernatural horror film *Poltergeist* (1982) when she was fatally strangled by her ex-boyfriend. Dunne grew up in a showbiz family that included her father, writer Dominick Dunne, her brother, actor Griffin Dunne, and her aunt and uncle, novelists Gregory Dunne and Joan Didion. Her killer spent less than four years in prison for her murder. Dunne is buried only a short distance away from Heather O'Rourke, who also died young after starring in *Poltergeist*. Because of their tragic deaths, *Poltergeist* has earned the reputation of being a "cursed film." Dunne is pictured at the far right in this still from *Poltergeist*.

RONALD HUGHES (1935–1970). Attorney Ronald Hughes disappeared in 1970 while representing Charles Manson Family member Leslie Van Houten during the Tate-LaBianca murder trial. Hughes was on a camping trip during a recess in the trial and failed to return to court when the trial resumed. His badly decomposed remains were discovered several months later. Although the cause of death was officially listed as "undetermined," Manson is believed by many to have ordered Hughes's murder in retaliation for his strategy of attempting to pin the blame for the Tate-LaBianca killings solely on him. Pictured at left is Charles Manson, the man who may be responsible for Hughes's death.

NADER NADERPOUR (1929–2000). An Iranian-born poet who was part of the New Persian Poetry movement, Nader Naderpour began his poetry career in the 1940s and continued writing until his death. His poems have been translated into English, French, German, and Italian. He also penned scholarly papers on Iran's politics, history, and culture. Naderpour was nominated for the Nobel Prize in Literature and received a Hellman-Hammett Grant from Human Rights Watch. (Photograph by E.J. Stephens.)

ROBERT NEWTON (1905–1956), URN GARDEN. Robert Newton began his career as a stage performer in London's West End in the 1920s. He gained attention for early film roles in *The Happy Breed* (1944) and Laurence Olivier's film version of *Henry V* the same year. His most famous role was in Disney's *Treasure Island* from 1950, in which he played Long John Silver. He continued acting in other pirate films, portraying the title character in *Blackbeard the Pirate* (1952). His performances became the model for how to portray a pirate to such an extent that he is considered the "patron saint" of International Talk Like a Pirate Day. Newton (below) is seen with child star Bobby Driscoll in *Treasure Island*.

ROY ORBISON (1936–1988). One of the pioneers of rock 'n' roll, Roy Orbison was an accomplished singer, guitar player, and songwriter, with a six-decade spanning career. The Texas-born performer mixed rockabilly, country and western, the blues, and rock with his mournful and haunting vocals to create a sound that was uniquely his own. In the early 1960s, Orbison released 22 Billboard Top 40 hit songs, most of which he wrote or cowrote. Some of his hits included "Only the Lonely," "Crying," "In Dreams," and "Oh, Pretty Woman." After this initial period of success, his popularity faded until the 1980s, when many of his songs were covered by other performers and used in popular movies.

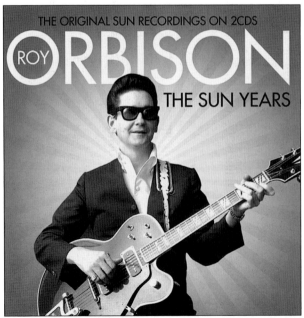

ROY ORBISON (1936–1988). During the 1980s, Roy Orbison joined the supergroup The Travelling Wilburys. One month after his death, his new single "You Got It" was released and became his first solo Billboard Top 10 hit in two decades. Orbison had many honors during his career including induction into the Songwriters Hall of Fame, the Nashville Songwriters Hall of Fame, and the Rock and Roll Hall of Fame. He was also the recipient of five Grammy Awards and a Grammy Lifetime Achievement Award. *Rolling Stone* magazine ranked him at number 37 on its "100 Greatest Artists of All Time" list and 13th on its list of the "100 Greatest Singers of All Time." His grave is unmarked. Above is a publicity shot of the band The Traveling Wilburys with, from left to right, Bob Dylan, Jeff Lynne, Tom Petty, Roy Orbison, and George Harrison.

GREGOR PIATIGORSKY (1903–1976). Gregor Piatigorsky was a Russian-born cellist who was considered one of the best string players of all time. He was also a composer, an educator, and an author. Many composers created works for him including cello concertos by Sergei Prokofiev, Paul Hindemith, Westwood neighbor Mario Castelnuovo-Tedesco, William Walton, and Vernon Duke. Piatigorsky collaborated with Igor Stravinsky on the arrangement of the "Suite Italienne" from the ballet *Pulcinella*. He owned two Stradivarius cellos and the famous 1739 Domenico Montagnana cello known as "Sleeping Beauty." His autobiography, *Cellist*, published in 1965, was popular with both readers and critics. Pictured are the graves of Piatigorsky and his wife, Jacqueline, who was a member of the Rothschild banking family. (Photograph by E.J. Stephens.)

FRANK PIERSON (1925–2012). Screenwriter Frank Pierson served in World War II then graduated from Harvard and became a correspondent for *Time* and *Life* magazines. His first Hollywood job was as a script editor on the television show *Have Gun–Will Travel*. He later wrote for *Naked City* and *Route 66*. His screenplays include *Cat Ballou* (1965) and *Cool Hand Luke* (1967), both of which were nominated for Academy Awards. Pierson later won the Oscar for his script for *Dog Day Afternoon* in 1975. Pierson served as the head of the Writers Guild of America and as the president of the Academy of Motion Picture Arts and Sciences. Above is a still from *Dog Day Afternoon*, starring Al Pacino.

DONNA REED (1921–1986). Donna Reed appeared in numerous films and television shows, but she is best remembered for one enduring film role, along with starring in her own show on television. Reed began appearing in films in the early 1940s, but her role as Jimmy Stewart's wife, Mary, in *It's a Wonderful Life* in 1946 is what she is most fondly remembered for today. In 1953, she appeared in a very different type of role as Montgomery Clift's girlfriend in *From Here to Eternity*, for which she received an Academy Award nomination. Her most popular role on television was in the hugely successful *The Donna Reed Show*, which ran from 1958 to 1966. Reed was nominated four times for Emmys and received a Golden Globe for her performance in the show. She continued to act into the 1980s, with her last big role coming in the 1984–1985 season of *Dallas*, where she replaced Barbara Bel Geddes as Miss Ellie Ewing.

ERNEST SCHOEDSACK (1883–1979) AND RUTH ROSE SCHOEDSACK (1896–1978), URN GARDEN. Ernest Schoedsack was a film director, producer, and cinematographer who learned his craft as a cameraman for Mack Sennett comedies before serving with the Signal Corps during World War I. After the war, he partnered with Merian C. Cooper to make several films, including *Chang: A Drama of the Wilderness* (1927), *The Most Dangerous Game* (1932), and *King Kong* (1933). His directing career continued with films such as *Son of Kong* (1933), *Dr. Cyclops* (1940), *The Monkey's Paw* (1948), and *Mighty Joe Young* (1949). He was forced to retire from making films due to deteriorating eyesight caused by an injury he received in the war. Coincidentally, just as Schoedsack specialized in directing films about giant apes, his wife, Ruth Rose, had a thing for writing them. She was working on an expedition for the New York Geographical Society when the couple first met. At the time, Cooper was struggling to get the script for his film about a romance between a young woman and a giant ape to work. Rose wrote a version that served as the basis for *King Kong*. Rose continued to write scripts in the same vein, including *Son of Kong, She* (1935), *The Last Days of Pompeii* (1935), and *Mighty Joe Young*, which was her final screenplay. She later served as a script doctor, doing rewrites and dialogue enhancements on scripts for which she rarely got screen credit.

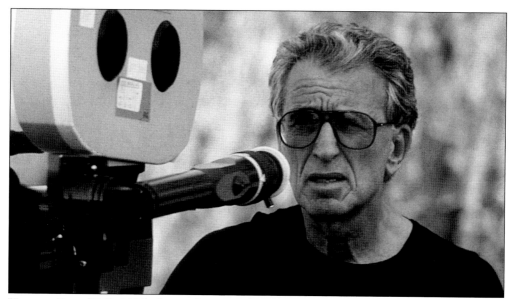

HERBERT ROSS (1927–2001). Actor, choreographer, producer, and director Herbert Ross directed the musical *Goodbye, Mr. Chips* in 1969. This was followed by *The Owl and the Pussycat* (1970), *Play It Again, Sam* (1972), *Funny Lady* (1975), and *The Turning Point* (1977). Ross directed Neil Simon's film version of *The Sunshine Boys* in 1975 followed by *The Goodbye Girl* (1977), *California Suite* (1978), *I Ought to Be in Pictures* (1982), and *Max Dugan Returns* (1983). During his later career, Ross had huge hits with the films *Footloose* (1984), *The Secret of My Success* (1987), and *Steel Magnolias* (1989). Ross worked closely with Westwood neighbor Ray Stark for several years.

IRENE TEDROW (1907–1995), URN GARDEN. Irene Tedrow was a popular actress who was active on both the stage and on television. She studied acting in England at the Memorial Theater at Stratford-on-Avon before moving to New York City to tour nationally with Maurice Evans's troupe. She began her television career in 1949 and appeared regularly on the popular television shows *The Addams Family*, *Maverick*, *Dennis the Menace*, *The Real McCoys*, *Rawhide*, *The Twilight Zone*, *The Andy Griffith Show*, *Wagon Train*, and *Leave it to Beaver*. She earned a Best Supporting Actress Emmy for her performance in *Eleanor and Franklin*. She is seen at right in an unidentified production.

FRANK TUTTLE (1892–1963).
Frank Tuttle was a Hollywood film director whose career began in the silent era and continued until 1959. He was a Yale graduate who worked in advertising before moving to Hollywood. His career in America came to a halt when he was labeled a Communist by the House Un-American Activities Committee (HUAC) in 1947 for his previous membership in the American Communist Party. He made a film in France before returning to the United States, where his career resumed after he agreed to give names of other suspected communists to HUAC. One of his final films was *A Cry in the Night* (1956), which starred Westwood neighbor Natalie Wood.

CORNEL WILDE (1912–1989). Cornel Wilde began his acting career on Broadway before transitioning into bit parts in small films. He later signed with 20th Century Fox and by 1945 was a major leading man. Wilde is best known for swashbuckling roles, playing Aladdin in *A Thousand and One Nights* (1945) and the son of Robin Hood in *The Bandit of Sherwood Forest* (1946). He also appeared in *A Song to Remember* (1945), for which he earned a nomination from the Academy for Best Actor. Wilde died of leukemia in 1989. Above, Wilde stands between Phil Silvers and Evelyn Keyes in a scene from *A Thousand and One Nights*.

NATALIE WOOD (1938–1981). Academy Award nominee Natalie Wood was born Natalie Zacharenko in San Francisco. She began acting at the age of four and landed a role in *Miracle on 34th Street* (1947) when she was eight. She is best known for her roles in *Rebel Without a Cause* (1955), *West Side Story* (1961), and *Splendor in the Grass* (1961), for which she was nominated for Best Actress opposite Warren Beatty (whom she later dated). Wood appeared in 56 films before dying under mysterious circumstances in 1981 on third husband Robert Wagner's yacht during a weekend trip to Santa Catalina Island. Her cause of death was originally said to be drowning before later being changed to "drowning and other undetermined factors," after it was "not clearly established" how Wood ended up in the water.

DARRYL F. ZANUCK (1902–1979) AND VIRGINIA ZANUCK (1906–1982). Darryl Zanuck began life in the tiny town of Wahoo, Nebraska. He joined the Army at the age of 14 after lying about his age and served in France during World War I. After the war, he returned to the United States and began writing stories for Mack Sennett and several scripts starring the heroic German Shepherd Rin Tin Tin for Warner Bros. He later left Warner Bros. over a salary dispute and partnered with Joseph Schenk to form 20th Century Pictures, creating the most successful independent movie studio of its time. The pair later acquired Fox Studios to form 20th Century Fox. A controversial figure, Zanuck is credited with popularizing the Golden Era of Hollywood's "casting couch culture." Zanuck is buried with his wife, silent film star Virginia Fox, who starred opposite Buster Keaton in several films.

FRANK ZAPPA (1940–1993). American cultural icon Frank Vincent Zappa was a prolific musician, composer, and leader of the rock band The Mothers of Invention. A master at mixing virtuosity, free-form improvisation, and biting comedic satire, Zappa's eclectic taste in music began in high school when he wrote classical music at the same time as playing rhythm and blues. He later took up the electric guitar, which was the beginning of a unique style of rock with lyrics heavily influenced by political and social factors.

FRANK ZAPPA (1940–1993).
Frank Zappa was well known as a passionate advocate for freedom of speech and against censorship and for his ironic comical lyrics, which made him the "godfather" of comedy rock. His four children—Moon Unit, Dweezil, Ahmet, and Diva—have become celebrities in their own right. Zappa, whose fans have erected statues of him in the cities of Baltimore and Vilnius, Lithuania, ironically rests under an unmarked grave.

Four

SECTION 4

Section 4, which is the area or lawn to the right of the large tree near Natalie Wood's grave, contains dozens of people who made names for themselves in entertainment and other industries.

In this section, be on the lookout for some lesser-known names like actress Norma Crane, who played Golde in *Fiddler on the Roof* (1971). She is buried near the grave of her friend Natalie Wood. Terry Leslie McQueen, Steve McQueen's daughter, is nearby. Edmund Di Giulio, who developed the Steadicam, is here near the graves of Jeanne Martin, Dean's wife, and actor Ed Lauter, whose monument reads like a movie poster.

Models Bettie Page and Dorothy Stratten are here, as is Stratten's former boyfriend, director Peter Bogdanovich. Clustered together under small markers by another large tree are Burt Lancaster, Eve Arden, Will and Ariel Durant, Brooks West, and Harold Hecht. Paul Gleason, Carl Wilson, Richard Anderson, Allan Melvin, and Minnie Riperton are close by.

Along the south curb, look for the row of graves that includes musician Ray Conniff, screenwriter Ernest Lehman, producer G. David Schine, and Jeff Morris, whose marker states that he was a "Fine Actor, Weather Permitting."

RICHARD ANDERSON (1926–2017). Actor Richard Anderson made frequent appearances on television during the 1970s playing Oscar Goldman, the boss of both Lee Majors on *Six Million Dollar Man* and Lindsay Wagner on *The Bionic Woman*. Anderson was married for a time to Katherine Thalberg, the daughter of legendary producer Irving Thalberg and actress Norma Shearer.

EVE ARDEN (1908–1990). Wisecracking Eve Arden sparkled on radio, stage, film, and television for decades. Born Eunice Quedens in the Bay Area, she received a Best Supporting Actress nomination for *Mildred Pierce* in 1945, which led to her enormously popular radio show, *Our Miss Brooks*. Actor Hy Averback, who was a regular on the program, is buried nearby. Arden became familiar to a new generation of moviegoers when she appeared as Principal McGee in *Grease* (1978) and its sequel. She is buried next to her husband, Brooks West, and agent-producer Harold Hecht.

PETER BOGDANOVICH (1939–2022). The legendary Peter Bogdanovich had a remarkable 60-year career in Hollywood as an actor, screenwriter, producer, historian, and director. He made his directorial debut in 1968 with the film *Targets*. The following decades he helmed such films as *The Last Picture Show* (1971), which earned him Best Director and Best Adapted Screenplay nominations, along with classics *What's Up, Doc?* (1972), *Paper Moon* (1973), and *Mask* (1985). Bogdanovich passed away in 2022 from Parkinson's disease and is buried next to his one-time girlfriend, Dorothy Stratten.

RAY CONNIFF (1916–2002).
Musician Ray Conniff became famous as the bandleader of The Ray Conniff Singers in the 1960s, who sold over 70 million records. After serving in the Army in World War II, Conniff worked for Columbia Records arranging compositions for many of the leading singers of the day. He created The Ray Conniff Singers as a choral group in 1959 with 12 women and 13 men. They had their biggest hit in 1966 with "Somewhere My Love," with lyrics put to "Lara's Theme" from the film *Doctor Zhivago* (1965). Conniff's grave marker is inscribed with the first four notes of this song.

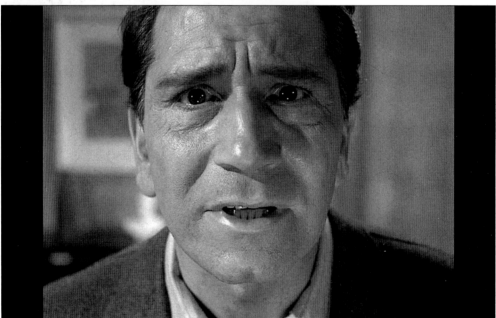

RICHARD CONTE (1910–1975). American actor Richard Conte appeared in more than 100 films over a 30-year career. He was discovered by director Elia Kazan and actor John Garfield when he was working as a singing waiter. Conte signed a contract with 20th Century Fox where he and Westwood neighbor Marilyn Monroe filmed their first screen tests together. Two of his first films were directed by Westwooder Lewis Milestone. He often appeared in heavy roles like in *The Godfather* (1972). His grave at Westwood Cemetery, which is near Natalie Wood, lists his years of life as "1910–1975–?" perhaps conveying his belief in reincarnation. Conte is pictured above in an episode of *The Twilight Zone* from 1959.

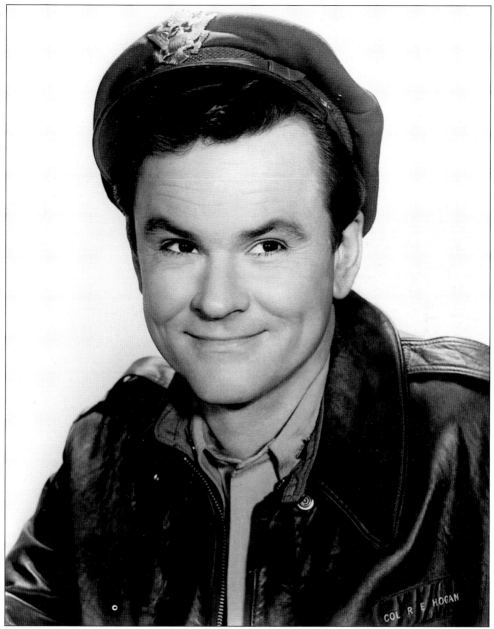

BOB CRANE (1928–1978). Actor Bob Crane is famous both for his role as Col. Robert Hogan on *Hogan's Heroes* and for the manner of his death. Crane was a popular disc jockey in Los Angeles who made the transition to television when he landed a role on *The Donna Reed Show* (Reed's grave is just to the south of Crane's). This led to his starring role in the comedy *Hogan's Heroes*, where he led a motley crew of prisoners in acts of espionage and sabotage from inside a German POW camp during World War II. His career floundered after the series was canceled in 1971. In June 1978, Crane was murdered in a motel in Scottsdale, Arizona, in a case that is still unsolved. Crane's controversial personal life was the subject of the film *Auto Focus* (2002), starring Greg Kinnear. Crane is buried with his second wife, Patricia Olson, who under the stage name Sigrid Valdis played Hilda on *Hogan's Heroes*. Richard Dawson, who also starred in the show, is buried nearby in Section 3.

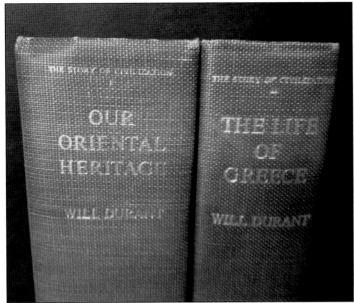

WILL DURANT (1885–1981) AND ARIEL DURANT (1898–1981). Historians Will and Ariel Durant are buried beside one another under a shady tree in Section 4. It is a lovely resting place for the two Pulitzer Prize and Presidential Medal of Freedom winners, who produced the massive 11-volume history of Eastern and Western cultures called *The Story of Civilization*, which took 40 years to complete. The Durants were married for 68 years and died within two weeks of one another.

GEOFF EMERICK (1945–2018). Geoff Emerick's name is familiar to Beatles fans "here, there, and everywhere" as the sound engineer and record producer who helped craft their sound on the albums *Revolver, Sgt. Pepper's Lonely Hearts Club Band*, and *Abbey Road*. When Emerick was 16, he landed an engineering job at EMI Studios in London where during the same week The Beatles recorded "Love Me Do." Emerick worked for the group off-and-on until their breakup in 1970. He also helped craft albums for Elvis Costello, America, Jeff Beck, Supertramp, and Cheap Trick. He also worked on several albums by Paul McCartney. In 2006, he wrote a controversial memoir about his time with The Beatles, called *Here, There and Everywhere*.

PAUL GLEASON (1939–2006). Actor Paul Gleason was a familiar face on television over a 40-year career, but he will be forever remembered as the authoritarian vice principal Richard "Dick" Vernon in the "Brat Pack" teen dramedy *The Breakfast Club* (1985). Gleason later spoofed this role in the 2001 comedy *Not Another Teen Movie*. Gleason's monument reads, "Actor/Ballplayer," which is true in both cases, as he spent two seasons in the Cleveland Indian's organization and played football for Florida State. Gleason died from lung cancer at age 67. Pictured from left to right are the "Brat Pack" from *The Breakfast Club*, Ally Sheedy, Judd Nelson, Anthony Michael Hall, Emilio Estevez, and Molly Ringwald.

LOUIS JOURDAN (1921–2015). Handsome French actor Louis Jourdan was known for playing suave characters in several films like *The Paradine Case* (1947), *Letter From an Unknown Woman* (1948), *Gigi* (1958), and *Octopussy* (1983). Jourdan's family was part of the French Resistance during World War II. Shortly after the end of hostilities, Jourdan married his wife, Berthe, who was known as "QuiQue." They would stay together for the remainder of their lives.

Burt Lancaster (1913–1994). Academy Award–winning legend Burt Lancaster was one of the most revered actors of his day. During a 45-year career, he starred in dozens of landmark films and became an accomplished producer as well. He began his career as a circus performer in the 1930s before starring in *The Killers* (1946), opposite Ava Gardner, which launched both of their careers. In 1953, Lancaster starred with Deborah Kerr in *From Here to Eternity*, which won the Best Picture Oscar, with Lancaster nominated for Best Actor. Four years later, he starred with Westwood neighbor Kirk Douglas in *Gunfight at the O.K. Corral*. Lancaster began producing films in the 1950s with his agent Harold Hecht (who is now buried just steps away). One was *Trapeze* (1956), where Lancaster got to put his circus performer skills on display. They also produced the classics *Sweet Smell of Success* (1957) and *Birdman of Alcatraz* (1962). Lancaster starred as a religious conman in *Elmer Gantry* in 1960, for which he won the Best Actor Oscar. He had a major hit with *Airport* (1970), which also starred Westwood neighbor Dean Martin. His last role was in *Field of Dreams* in 1989. Lancaster died from a heart attack at age 80 in 1994. His small plaque, pictured below in the foreground, sits in the law in Section 4. The graves of Hugh Hefner and Marilyn Monroe are visible at the upper-left of the photo.

ERNEST LEHMAN (1915–2005). Screenwriter Ernest Lehman began his writing career working for a publicity firm. This experience contributed to his screenplay for *Sweet Smell of Success* (1957), which is a film with connections to several Westwood residents. Lehman wrote the screenplays for *Sabrina* (1954), *North By Northwest* (1959), *West Side Story* (1961), *The Sound of Music* (1965), *Hello, Dolly!* (1969), and *Family Plot* (1976). The Academy of Motion Picture Arts and Sciences granted Lehman an honorary Oscar in 2001.

HARRY (1920–2013) AND MARILYN LEWIS (1929–2017). Supporting actor Harry Lewis enjoyed a steady career in films during the 1940s. In 1950, Lewis and his girlfriend (later wife) Marilyn pooled $3,500 to open a restaurant on the Sunset Strip called Hamburger Hamlet, which would eventually grow into a chain with 24 locations which the Lewises later sold for $30 million. In the late 1960s, Marilyn Lewis launched a line of clothing under the brand name Cardinali. Harry Lewis died in 2013 at age 93. Marilyn passed away four years later. Pictured above is the interior of the original Hamburger Hamlet on the Sunset Strip.

PORTLAND MASON SCHUYLER (1948–2004). Portland Mason Schuyler was a child actress who was the daughter of actors James and Pamela Mason. She was the sister of film producer Morgan Mason and sister-in-law to his wife, pop singer Belinda Carlisle. Schuyler's first television appearance was in an episode of the sitcom *The George Burns and Gracie Allen Show* at age six. Two years later, she played Gregory Peck's daughter in the classic film *The Man in the Grey Flannel Suit* (1956). She later became a writer and was working on a book about her father at the time of her death. (Photograph by E.J. Stephens.)

LLOYD NOLAN (1902–1985). Lloyd Nolan was a stage, film, and television actor who alternated between leading and character roles throughout a career that included over 150 screen credits. His first big impact was on stage in the Broadway hit *The Caine Mutiny Court-Martial*, in which he originated the role of Captain Queeg. He went on to win the 1955 Best Actor Emmy Award for reprising the role, when the play was televised. His career continued to thrive in the 1950s with roles in films like *A Tree Grows in Brooklyn* (1945) and *Peyton Place* (1957). Nolan's final role was in Woody Allen's *Hannah and Her Sisters* (1986), which was released a year after his death. Nolan is pictured above with Carole Landis in a still from *It Happened in Flatbush* (1942).

BETTIE PAGE (1923–2008). Model Bettie Page, the "Queen of Pinups," was born in Nashville in 1923. She graduated as the salutatorian of her high school, where she was voted "Girl Most Likely to Succeed." Page received a scholarship to college where she initially studied to be a teacher before switching to acting. In 1950, Page met New York Police Department officer Jerry Tibbs, who was also a photographer. Tibbs offered to help her develop a portfolio and suggested she grow bangs to cover her forehead, which became her iconic look. Throughout the 1950s, Page posed for mail-order photographs and specialty films in both the pinup and bondage styles. She also appeared in acting roles on television on *The Jackie Gleason Show* and on stage in Off-Broadway productions. Page also appeared in burlesque films such as *Teaserama* (1955), where she performed exotic dance routines. One of her photographers, Bunny Yeager, sent *Playboy* her photographs, and Hugh Hefner selected her to be the Playmate of the Month for the magazine's January 1955 issue. Today, she and Hef are buried within sight of one another.

MINNIE RIPERTON (1947–1979). Minnie Riperton was a soul singer known for her impressive five-octave voice and as an advocate in the fight against breast cancer. As a teen growing up in Chicago, Riperton was part of the girl group the Gems and provided backup vocals for artists including Etta James, Bo Diddley, and Chuck Berry. In 1970, she released her first solo album, *Come to My Garden*. Her second album, *Perfect Angel*, was released in 1974 and coproduced by Stevie Wonder. It sold more than a million copies and established Riperton as one of the era's best vocalists. In 2023, *Rolling Stone* magazine ranked her number 65 on the list of the "Greatest Singers of All Time." Riperton was married to songwriter and music producer Richard Rudolph. Together, they had two children, Marc and Maya. Marc became a music engineer, and Maya is an actress and comedienne who has starred on *Saturday Night Live* and in many other film and television shows. Riperton succumbed to breast cancer in 1979 at age 31.

DOROTHY STRATTEN (1960–1980). Dorothy Stratten, *Playboy's* 1980 Playmate of the Year, was tragically murdered at the young age of 20 by her husband and manager, Paul Snider (pictured above with Stratten). She was still married to Snider when she fell in love with director Peter Bogdanovich while the two worked together on the film *They All Laughed* (1981). Stratten was planning to leave Snider when she visited him at his townhouse to finalize the financial terms of their divorce. An enraged Snider killed Stratten with a shotgun before turning the gun on himself.

DOROTHY STRATTEN (1960–1980). Dorothy Stratten was the subject of two films, *Death of a Centerfold: The Dorothy Stratten Story* (1981) and *Star 80* (1983), and is a recurring character in the Hulu miniseries *Welcome to Chippendales*. In an interesting twist, Bogdanovich, pictured with Stratten and now buried at her side, married Stratten's younger sister, Louise, in 1988.

DANNY SUGERMAN (1954–2005). Danny Sugerman, the "Number-One Doors fan of the World," became the manager of the legendary rock group following the death of Jim Morrison in 1971. He penned several books about the band, including *No One Here Gets Out Alive*. Sugerman later managed Iggy Pop and Ray Manzarek's solo career. In 1993, Sugerman married Fawn Hall, who became famous during the controversial Iran-Contra Affair. Sugerman reportedly found solace from heroin addiction through Buddhism before dying in 2005 in Los Angeles from lung cancer.

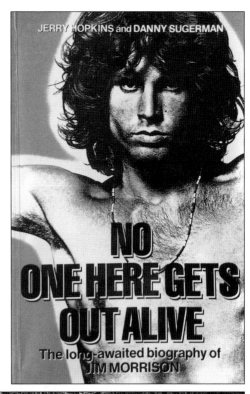

RENATA VANNI (1909–2004) AND DELIA SALVI (1927–2015). Mother and daughter actresses Renata Vanni and Delia Salvi rest together under a single headstone near the curb at the southern end of the section. Italian native Vanni was a familiar face on television during the 1960s, after having appeared in such notable films as *Three Coins in the Fountain* (1954), which starred Westwood neighbor Louis Jourdan, *The Greatest Story Ever Told* (1965), and *A Patch of Blue* (1965). Delia Salvi, Vanni's daughter, followed her mother into acting, landing her first role in *From Here to Eternity* (1953), which starred Westwooder Burt Lancaster. She studied acting under Lee Strasberg at The Actors Studio in New York and later became a noted acting teacher herself after earning her PhD from UCLA in 1969. Salvi continued acting while simultaneously serving as a professor of theatre arts until her 2011 retirement.

CARL WILSON (1946–1998). Carl Wilson, along with brothers Brian and Dennis, cofounded the legendary sibling surf band known as The Beach Boys. Wilson was the band's leader and lead guitarist, and his voice is the clear soprano featured on many popular songs, including "Good Vibrations" and "Kokomo." He became ill in 1997 at his vacation home in Hawaii and was diagnosed with lung cancer. Carl's brother, Dennis, who drowned in 1983, had a brief friendship with infamous cult leader Charles Manson. At live shows, Wilson always dedicated the song "Heaven" to Dennis. Carl died in 1998, just two months after his mother, Audree Wilson, passed away. She is buried nearby in the Gardens of Serenity. When not creating music, Wilson was a member of a religious group known as the Movement of Spiritual Inner Awareness. Pictured above, from left to right, are Carl Wilson, Brian Wilson, Al Jardine, Dennis Wilson, and Mike Love.

Five

SECTION 5

The next phase of the tour takes us to the far northwest corner of the cemetery. This L-shaped grassy plot begins at the ivy-covered wall at the far left by the entry gate and extends to the wall of crypts to the right.

Straight ahead near the north wall is a white mausoleum that contains the remains of oilman and philanthropist Armand Hammer and his family. Close to the Hammer mausoleum are the graves of actress Eva Gabor and noted filmmaker John Cassavetes. Nearby is Franklin Schaffner, who won a Best Director Oscar for 1970's *Patton*. Close to the curb is the grave of Loretta Funk Hadler, who appeared in boyfriend Ed Wood's Z-picture *The Bride of the Monster* in 1955 and did not seem to mind having that fact placed on her marker. Closer to the curb is the beautiful bronze plaque bequeathed to funnyman Don Knotts by his fans. To the right, where the lawn narrows, are the graves of Hollywood super-agent Swifty Lazar and jazz singing superstar Mel Tormé.

On the wall of crypts to the right in the tiny area known as Sunset Terrance is the crypt of writer Truman Capote, who is entombed with Johnny Carson's former wife, Joanne. On the same wall is novelist Jackie Collins, who sold over a half-billion copies of her steamy novels. She shares a crypt with her husband, Oscar Lerman, who turned several of his wife's books into feature films. The crypt of child star Heather O'Rourke is at the far right on the bottom row. At one time, Rat Packer Peter Lawford's body occupied a crypt above her but was later removed. For a time, Jack Lemmon's body occupied Lawford's former crypt before being reburied on the opposite side of the cemetery.

Truman Capote (1924–1984), Sunshine Terrace Crypts. Author Truman Capote was born Truman Streckfus Persons in New Orleans and raised in Alabama and New York City. Capote is most famous for his novella *Breakfast at Tiffany's* from 1958 and his true-crime novel *In Cold Blood* (1966), which were both later made into highly acclaimed films. One of Capote's best friends was *To Kill A Mockingbird* author Harper Lee, who he used as the model for the character Idabel in his novel *Other Voices, Other Rooms* (1948). Lee returned the favor by modeling the character Dill in *To Kill A Mockingbird* after Capote. Capote died at the home of his friend Joanne Carson (the ex-wife of Johnny Carson), and his name appears on her crypt. It is unclear if his ashes were actually placed here. Some reports claim they were scattered while others say they were sold at auction.

JOHN CASSAVETES (1929–1989). *The New Yorker* once called John Cassavetes "perhaps the most influential American director of the last half century." While starring in several notable films in the 1950s and 1960s, like *Edge of the City* (1957), *The Killers* (1964), *The Dirty Dozen* (1967), and *Rosemary's Baby* (1968), Cassavetes taught an acting style that emphasized creative joy in contrast to the more established method acting style that was popular at the time. He began writing, producing, and directing his own features with *Shadows* (1959). Much of his work was done outside of the major Hollywood studios, helping to legitimize independent filmmaking. Cassavetes was nominated for an Oscar (his first of three) for writing the film *Faces* (1968), which featured his wife, Gina Rowlands (pictured together above). He began working regularly with actors Ben Gazzara and Westwood neighbor Peter Falk in 1970's *Husbands*. Cassavetes was nominated for another Oscar for directing *A Woman Under the Influence* (1974), which starred Rowlands. He made *The Killing of a Chinese Bookie*, starring Gazzara, in 1976, and *Opening Night* with Gazzara and Rowlands the following year. Cassavetes continued making films until his death at age 59 in 1989 from cirrhosis of the liver. He is buried beside his mother-in-law, actress Lady Rowlands.

JACKIE COLLINS (1937–2015), SUNSHINE TERRACE CRYPTS. British romance novelist Jackie Collins wrote 32 novels during her career, and each became a *New York Times* best seller. The younger sister of actress Joan Collins, her books sold over 500 million copies in forty languages. Collins was the daughter of a theatrical agent who represented Tom Jones, Shirley Bassey, and The Beatles. After a few years spent acting in British productions, Collins wrote her first bestseller in 1968, entitled *The World Is Full of Married Men*. The salacious nature of the novel got it banned in South Africa and Australia, which only added to its popularity. After a move to Los Angeles, Collins wrote her most successful novel in 1983 called *Hollywood Wives*, which became a television miniseries. Collins maintained a prolific writing schedule until her death from breast cancer in 2015. She is buried with her second husband, American nightclub owner Oscar Lerman, who died in 1992 from prostate cancer. Lerman helped turn several of his wife's novels into films.

EVA GABOR (1919–1995). The youngest of the three Hungarian Gabor sisters, beautiful, blonde Eva Gabor appeared in several films during a 50-year career, but she will be most remembered for her role as Lisa Douglas on television's *Green Acres*. Acting opposite Westwood resident Eddie Albert, Gabor played a big-city socialite who is forced to adjust to rural life after her husband decides to quit his job as a high-priced New York attorney to become a gentleman farmer. Gabor provided the voices for Disney's features *The Aristocats* (1970), *The Rescuers* (1977), and *The Rescuers Down Under* (1990). Above, from left to right, are the three Gabor sisters, Zsa Zsa, Eva, and Magda. Eva's five marriages were fewer in number than those of Zsa Zsa (nine) and Magda (six).

ARMAND HAMMER (1898–1990). The founder of Occidental Petroleum, Armand Hammer, and the baking soda company, Arm & Hammer, were both named after the "arm and hammer" emblem that represents the god Vulcan, which is a symbol for industry. Hammer was asked so often about his name and the baking soda brand that he eventually became a minority owner of the company. Hammer created the Armand Hammer Museum (pictured at right) a block north of his grave to display his precious art. Actor Armie Hammer is Hammer's great-grandson.

DON KNOTTS (1924–2006).
Although Don Knotts starred in such notable comedies as *The Incredible Mr. Limpet* (1964), *The Ghost and Mr. Chicken* (1966), and *Pleasantville* (1998), to the millions of visitors to the imaginary town of Mayberry in TV land, Knotts will always be bumbling deputy Barney Fife. Knotts was born in West Virginia in 1924 and began his career in show business as a ventriloquist. He appeared alongside Andy Griffith in the film *No Time for Sergeants* in 1958, which began a lifelong friendship and professional relationship between the two men. Knotts, as Deputy Fife, is seen at left with Griffith in a publicity photo from *The Andy Griffith Show*.

DON KNOTTS (1924–2006). In 162 hilarious episodes of *The Andy Griffith Show*, Knotts played Deputy Fife, ineptly patrolling Mayberry armed only with a single bullet and a Napoleon complex. Coincidentally, Knotts died on the same day as Dennis Weaver, who also reached stardom playing a deputy on television. For many years, Knotts was buried under a simple headstone. His fans later purchased the ornate bronze marker depicting some of his most famous roles that we see today. In this photograph, Knotts's grave is in the foreground with the mausoleum of Armand Hammer behind.

SWIFTY LAZAR (1907–1993). Five-foot, four-inch dealmaker and super-agent Irving Lazar began representing vaudevillians in the 1930s. He went to Hollywood where Humphrey Bogart gave him his nickname after he put together three major deals for "Bogie" in one day. Lazar represented dozens of Hollywood's biggest stars, including Westwood neighbors Walter Matthau and Truman Capote, who is buried in a crypt just a few feet away. Lazar married model Mary Van Nuys, who was 25 years his junior, in 1963. The Lazars hosted a post-Oscars party that was the most sought-after invitation in Hollywood. In the 1970s, Lazar helped several actors sell their memoirs, including Westwooder Kirk Douglas. Lazar is pictured here with actress Polly Bergen.

Carol Anne Freeling (Heather O'Rourke) screams for her parents when violent supernatural spirits attempt to capture her in MGM's "Poltergeist," a science-horror story produced by Steven Spielberg and Frank Marshall. Tobe Hooper directed from a screenplay by Steven Spielberg, Michael Grais & Mark Victor. The film will be released in the United States and Canada by MGM/United Artists Distribution and Marketing.

HEATHER O'ROURKE (1975–1988), SUNSHINE TERRACE CRYPTS. Heather O'Rourke was a child actress best known for her role as Carol Anne in the three *Poltergeist* films. She was also a television star with recurring roles on the sitcoms *Happy Days* and *Webster*. Heather was nominated for six Young Artist Awards between 1983 and 1987, winning Best Performance by a Young Actress in a Television Show in 1985 for her role on *Webster*. O'Rourke died of cardiac arrest at age 12 caused by congenital stenosis of the intestine and septic shock. Her line "They're here!" from the first *Poltergeist* film in 1982 was voted number 69 on the American Film Institute's "100 Movie Quotes" list in 2005. O'Rourke is pictured above in a still from *Poltergeist*.

WELCOME HOME   Director FRANKLIN J. SCHAFFNER on the set of his final film, "Welcome Home".

FRANKLIN SCHAFFNER (1920–1989). Academy Award–winning director Franklin Schaffner served in the US Navy in World War II and later landed a job as an assistant director for *The March of Time* documentary film series. In 1955, he directed the original television version of *Twelve Angry Men*, for which he won an Emmy Award. He won another Emmy the following year for *The Caine Mutiny Court-Martial* and a third for his work on the drama series *The Defenders* in 1962. Moving to film, Schaffner directed the hugely successful *Planet of the Apes* in 1968. His next film was *Patton* (1970), which starred Westwood neighbor George C. Scott. The film won several Academy Awards including Best Picture, Best Actor for Scott (which he declined), and Best Director for Schaffner (which he kept). Schaffner had later success with *Nicholas and Alexandra* (1971), *Papillon* (1973), and *The Boys from Brazil* (1978). He served as president of the Directors Guild of America from 1987 until his death.

MEL TORMÉ (1925–1999). Mel Tormé, the Grammy Award–winning singer nicknamed "The Velvet Fog," was a multitalented musician, actor, drummer, author, and pioneer of cool jazz. He began writing music at age 13 and eventually composed over 250 songs, including the music for "The Christmas Song" (more commonly known as "Chestnuts Roasting on an Open Fire") in 1946. After appearing on screen in a 1947 musical, Tormé became a teen idol. He would go on to perform for decades with many of the most revered stars in the genre and influenced later bands like The Manhattan Transfer and The Four Freshmen. One of his many notable television appearances was as Harry Anderson's guardian angel on *Night Court*. Anderson's character was portrayed as a devoted Mel Tormé fan, which was true of Anderson in real life, confirmed when he was asked to deliver the eulogy at Tormé's funeral in 1999. Tormé had ties to many of his fellow Westwooders. He wrote a biography about his friend and Westwood neighbor Buddy Rich in 1991 and claimed that one of his favorite vocalists was Patty Andrews, of the Andrews Sisters, who is buried a few hundred feet to the south. A little-known fact about Tormé was that he was a real-life quick draw expert.

Six

SECTION 6

Section 6, the last portion of the tour, consists of the row of white outdoor crypts on the north side of the cemetery. These walls house three sanctuaries: Tenderness, Devotion, and Tranquility. Inside the Sanctuary of Tenderness are the crypts of tunesmith Harry Warren, actor Christopher George, writer Sidney Sheldon, Panavision head Robert Gottschalk, and director Lewis Milestone. Next door, in the Sanctuary of Devotion, are the crypts of attorney-to-the-stars Greg Bautzer, art director Edward Carrere, actress Dorothy Patrick, and actor Whit Bissell. Bissell appeared in the monster-horror classic *Creature from the Black Lagoon* in 1954. In another example of Westwood's interesting connections, *Lagoon* was directed by Jack Arnold, whose monument is on the opposite side of the cemetery, and written by Harry Essex, who is also buried nearby. Film editor Louis Loeffler and *Lost In Space* alum Jonathon Harris are here as well. MGM portrait specialist Clarence Bull, who was Greta Garbo's favorite photographer, is also here, as is Richard Murrow, who built Howard Hughes's *Spruce Goose* airplane.

In the Sanctuary of Tranquility are the crypts of screenwriter Nunnally Johnson, actor Philip Dorn, opera star Miliza Korjus, drummer Buddy Rich, cinematographer James Wong Howe, voice actress June Foray, and singer Eileen Barton.

Section 6 ends just before the wall of crypts that are adjacent to the tomb of Marilyn Monroe, which brings this tour full circle. Even though the cemetery existed for six decades before Marilyn's passing, her star power was such that virtually everyone highlighted within these pages chose Westwood as their final resting site after her death in 1962.

GREG BAUTZER (1911–1987), SANCTUARY OF DEVOTION. Attorney-to-the-stars Greg Bautzer is interred in the Sanctuary of Devotion. During a long and tumultuous career in Hollywood, Bautzer represented such personalities as Howard Hughes, Kirk Kerkorian, Ginger Rogers, Ingrid Bergman, Joan Crawford, and Westwood resident James Aubrey. Known as much for his romantic dalliances as for his courtroom maneuvering, Bautzer (pictured above with Ginger Rogers) was married four times and had relationships with actresses Barbara Payton, Dorothy Lamour, Lana Turner, and Joan Crawford. Bautzer died of heart failure (and possibly exhaustion) in 1987.

EDWARD CARRERE (1906–1984), SANCTUARY OF DEVOTION. Art directors are responsible for the overall look of a film and decide how to present visual images to best tell the story. For over 30 years, Mexican-born Edward Carrere was one of the best in the business. The first of his three Academy Award nominations came in 1949 for *The Adventures of Don Juan*. He earned another in 1960 for *Sunrise at Campobello* and took home the Oscar seven years later for *Camelot*. Carrere worked on such notable productions as *White Heat* (1949), *The Fountainhead* (1949), and *Dial M for Murder* (1954). He also worked on *Sweet Smell of Success* (1957), with Westwood neighbors Burt Lancaster, Alexander Mackendrick, James Wong Howe, Ernest Lehman, and Harold Hecht. He again worked with Burt Lancaster in 1960 on *Elmer Gantry*.

JUNE FORAY (1917–2017), SANCTUARY OF TRANQUILITY. Some of the television and movie stars who are now housed in Westwood Cemetery were more famous for their voices than for their faces. This is the case with voice actress June Foray, who over the course of a long career voiced such memorable cartoon characters as Rocket J. Squirrel, Natasha Fatale, and Nell Fenwick on *The Rocky and Bullwinkle Show*. Foray also voiced several other characters, including Granny and Witch Hazel for Warner Bros., Lucifer the Cat for Disney's *Cinderella*, and a host of characters for Walter Lantz's *Woody Woodpecker* cartoons. Foray also provided the voice of Cindy Lou Who in *How the Grinch Stole Christmas*, and for Mattel's Chatty Cathy doll. Often compared to the great voice actor Mel Blanc, cartoon director Chuck Jones was once quoted as saying, "June Foray is not the female Mel Blanc. Mel Blanc was the male June Foray."

CHRISTOPHER GEORGE (1931–1983), SANCTUARY OF TENDERNESS. Actor Christopher George is best remembered for his starring role on television's *The Rat Patrol*. George was born in Michigan to Greek immigrants and considered becoming a Greek Orthodox priest before turning to acting. In 1965, he made an appearance in the film *In Harm's Way* with Westwooder Kirk Douglas, where he met his boyhood idol John Wayne. The two became lifelong friends and costarred together in other Westerns. During a USO tour in 1967, George came under Viet Cong fire. George was married to actress Lynda Day (pictured at left) and the two often costarred together on TV. George posed nude in the June 1974 issue of *Playgirl* and was the uncle of *Wheel of Fortune*'s letter-turner, Vanna White.

JAMES WONG HOWE (1899–1976), SANCTUARY OF TRANQUILITY. Cinematographer James Wong Howe (pictured above in the center) was born in China and immigrated to the United States at the age of five. He began his film career as an assistant to Cecil B. DeMille during the silent era. Howe went on to earn ten Academy Award nominations, winning two statues. Howe famously crafted the use of dramatic lighting and deep shadows which created the classic film noir look. As a non-native, Howe often suffered from racism despite his success in Hollywood and only became a citizen after anti-immigration laws changed. Although he was married for many years to a white woman, antimiscegenation laws kept the union from being legally accepted in America until 1948. He continued working in Hollywood until shortly before his death in 1976.

NUNNALLY JOHNSON (1897–1977) AND DORRIS BOWDEN (1914–2005), SANCTUARY OF TRANQUILITY. Screenwriter Nunnally Johnson is buried with his wife, actress Dorris Bowden, in a small crypt in the Sanctuary of Tranquility. Johnson wrote over 50 screenplays during his career and is most famous for his Academy Award–nominated script for *The Grapes of Wrath* (1940). Johnson met Bowden on the set of that film, where she played the character Rosasharn. The previous year, she made appearances in *Young Mr. Lincoln* and *Drums Along the Mohawk*. (Photograph by Kim Stephens.)

LEWIS MILESTONE (1895–1980), SANCTUARY OF TENDERNESS. Lewis Milestone left Eastern Europe for America, arriving shortly after his 18th birthday. After a lengthy apprenticeship, Milestone directed *Seven Sinners* in 1925, which was written by Westwood neighbor Darryl F. Zanuck. Milestone won an Oscar in 1927 for *Two Arabian Knights* and made his masterpiece in 1930 with *All Quiet on the Western Front*, which starred Westwooder Lew Ayres. His career was almost derailed during Hollywood's Red Scare when he narrowly missed being blacklisted. In the 1960s, Milestone directed *Ocean's 11*, which costarred Westwood neighbor Dean Martin. Milestone had a stroke in 1978 shortly after the death of his wife of 43 years, Kendall Lee. He died two years later.

BUDDY RICH (1917–1987), SANCTUARY OF TRANQUILITY. Buddy Rich was a drummer, songwriter, and bandleader, famous for his outsized personality and influence on jazz. Rich began drumming at the age of two and by his early twenties was playing with the cream of the big band crop, including Tommy Dorsey, Count Basie, Artie Shaw, and Harry James. After serving in the Marines, he formed the Buddy Rich Orchestra, which lasted from 1945 through 1948. The group often played at the Apollo Theater and featured Frank Sinatra as the vocalist. Rich's drumming has appeared on over 100 albums. Some of the most popular and influential being *Krupa and Rich* (1955), Gene Krupa's *Swingin' New Big Band* (1966), and *Rich versus Roach*, featuring his then-rival, Max Roach. Rich also worked as a session drummer and backed famous performers like Ella Fitzgerald and Louis Armstrong and was often a guest on late-night television shows, particularly *The Tonight Show Starring Johnny Carson*. He is considered one of the best drummers of all time and was voted the 16th best drummer in a 2016 reader's poll by *Rolling Stone* magazine. Rich is interred in the Sanctuary of Tranquility. In the photo below, Rich's crypt is seen at the far right with the bouquet.

SIDNEY SHELDON (1917–2007), SANCTUARY OF TENDERNESS. A writer who produced plays, screenplays, and novels, Sidney Sheldon began his career writing musicals for Broadway in the 1940s and later won a Tony Award in 1959 for the musical *Redhead.* His success on stage brought him to Hollywood, where he wrote numerous scripts, including *The Bachelor and the Bobby-Soxer* in 1947, which earned him an Academy Award. Some of his other screenplay credits include *Easter Parade* (1948), *Annie Get Your Gun* (1950), and *Billy Rose's Jumbo* (1962). Sheldon then became a television writer and producer where he created many popular programs including *The Patty Duke Show, I Dream of Jeannie, Nancy,* and *Hart to Hart.* Sheldon wrote his first novel in 1969, *The Naked Face,* which was well received and earned him a nomination for Best First Novel from the Mystery Writers of America. This was followed by a series of best-sellers, including *The Other Side of Midnight, Windmills of the Gods* (pictured at right), *The Sands of Time,* and *The Doomsday Conspiracy.* In 2005, he wrote his autobiography, *The Other Side of Me,* which turned out to be his final book.

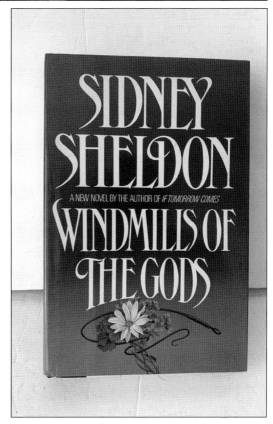

HARRY WARREN (1893–1981), SANCTUARY OF TENDERNESS. American national treasure Harry Warren was a songwriter and composer who was nominated for the Academy Award for Best Song 11 times and won three. During his lifetime he wrote over 800 songs with a majority composed for the screen. Warren's songs were featured in more than 300 movies and 112 of the Warner Bros. *Merrie Melodies* and *Looney Tunes* shorts. He wrote 21 songs that made it to number 1 on the *Your Hit Parade* radio program. (Photograph by E.J. Stephens.)

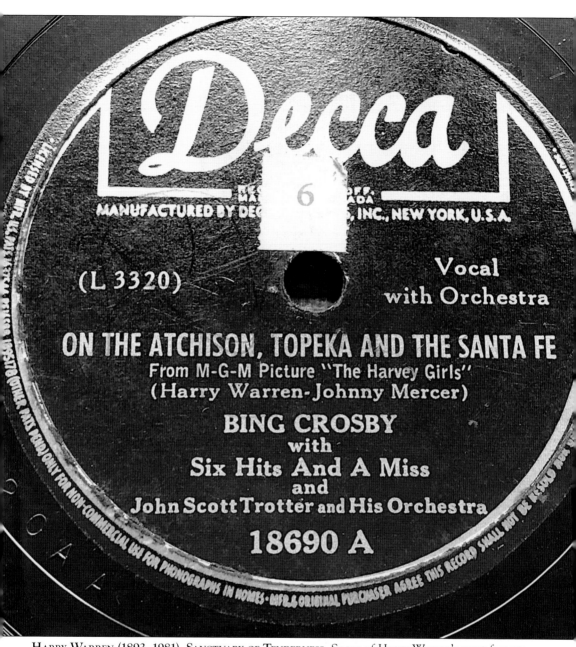

HARRY WARREN (1893–1981), SANCTUARY OF TENDERNESS. Some of Harry Warren's most famous works are "Chattanooga Choo-Choo," "I Only Have Eyes for You," "42nd Street," and "That's Amore." His three Oscar-winning songs were "Lullaby of Broadway" from *42nd Street* (1933), "You'll Never Know" from *Hello, Frisco, Hello* (1943), and "On the Atchison, Topeka, and the Santa Fe" from *The Harvey Girls* (1946). While perhaps not as well-known as some other songwriters, Warren composed as many hit songs as his more famous contemporaries Irving Berlin and Cole Porter.

Discover Thousands of Local History Books
Featuring Millions of Vintage Images

Arcadia Publishing, the leading local history publisher in the United States, is committed to making history accessible and meaningful through publishing books that celebrate and preserve the heritage of America's people and places.

Find more books like this at
www.arcadiapublishing.com

Search for your hometown history, your old stomping grounds, and even your favorite sports team.